MARRIAGE INTERRUPTED

ALSO BY JULIE PLAGENS

Estranged: Finding Hope When Your Family Falls Apart

Creating Family Memories: How to Make Family Time with a Crazy Schedule

MARRIAGE INTERRUPTED

How to Deal with Unexpected Conflict as a Couple and Stay in Love

JULIE PLAGENS

CREATIVE ENTERPRISES STUDIO

BEDFORD, TEXAS

Marriage Interrupted

Copyright © 2023 Julie Plagens.

All rights reserved. No portion of this book may be reproduced, stored in a retrieval system, or transmitted in any form or by any means—electronic, mechanical, photocopy, recording, scanning, or other—except for brief quotations in critical reviews or articles, or as specifically allowed by the U. S. Copyright Act of 1976, as amended, without the prior written permission of the publisher.

Published with assistance from Books, Bach & Beyond, Inc. d/b/a Creative Enterprises Studio, 1507 Shirley Way, Suite A, Bedford, TX 76022.

Unless otherwise noted, Scripture quotations are taken from the Holy Bible, New International Version®, NIV®. Copyright © 1973, 1978, 1984, 2011 by Biblica, Inc.® Used by permission of Zondervan. All rights reserved worldwide. www.zondervan.com. The "NIV" and "New International Version" are trademarks registered in the United States Patent and Trademark Office by Biblica, Inc.®

Scripture quotations marked AMP are taken from the Amplified® Bible. Copyright © 2015 by The Lockman Foundation, La Habra, CA 90631. All rights reserved. Used by permission. www.Lockman.org.

Scripture quotations marked GNT are taken from the Good News Translation® (Today's English Version, Second Edition) © 1992 American Bible Society. All rights reserved. Used by permission.

Scripture quotations marked HCSB are taken from the Holman Christian Standard Bible®. Copyright © 1999, 2000, 2002, 2003, 2009 by Holman Bible Publishers. Used by permission. HCSB® is a federally registered trademark of Holman Bible Publishers.

Scripture quotations marked NLT are taken from the Holy Bible, New Living Translation. Copyright © 1996, 2004, 2015 by Tyndale House Foundation. Used by permission of Tyndale House Publishers, Inc., Carol Stream, Illinois 60188. All rights reserved.

ISBNs:
  Softcover: 979-8-9876583-4-5

  e-Book: 979-8-9876583-5-2

  Library of Congress Control Number: 2023913564

23 24 25 26 27 28   6 5 4 3 2 1

This book is dedicated to my husband, Andy.

Thank you for loving me and believing in me, even when I didn't believe in myself.

I'm still madly in love with you.

TABLE OF CONTENTS

Join the Mom Remade Community	ix
Introduction	xi

PART I — Interrupted

Chapter	1.	Love at First Bite	3
Chapter	2.	The Revenge Muffins	13
Chapter	3.	Hard Endings Are Just Beginnings	23
Chapter	4.	A Job Well Done	33
Chapter	5.	The Disappearing Act	41
Chapter	6.	Marriage Interrupted	51

PART II — Redeemed

Chapter	7.	Through the Doors of Eden	63
Chapter	8.	People-Pleasing Pizza	83
Chapter	9.	Liar, Liar, Pants on Fire	99
Chapter	10.	Forgiving the Unforgettable	113
Chapter	11.	The Mouse That Changed Our House	133
Chapter	12.	How to Change Your Spouse	145
Chapter	13.	Dreams Do Come True	159

Appendix	169
Recommended Resources	179
Sources	181

JOIN THE MOM REMADE COMMUNITY

About five years ago, I dropped my last child off at college; it was a bittersweet moment. I was glad to release her into adulthood, but I was also sad because I was technically out of a job. I no longer had anyone at home who needed a full-time mom. On the long drive home, I asked God what He wanted me to do now that I was an empty nester. Unlike some of my prayers, this one God answered immediately.

His Spirit quietly spoke to me in the car that day. He said to tell other women about Him. It wasn't a big, loud voice; it was a sudden "knowing." Specifically, He said to tell women how to follow Him. Not how to be perfect, but just how to follow Him, especially through the hard times.

He reminded me of my struggles with marriage, parenting, and family and how much I have been encouraged by the testimonies of other authors who navigated difficult situations and have been willing to talk about it publicly. After that revelation in the car, I knew I needed to tell others what I had learned about being a young wife and mom and about my struggles with my family of origin. I figured if God was in it, someone would listen. Surely others have struggled with the same things I did.

Since then, I have written three books, been on multiple podcasts, spoken in public, maintained a blog, and sent out a newsletter when possible. My mission has been to provide a place online where other women can find marriage and family support that offers hope and healing.

INTRODUCTION

Do you ever wonder what your life would have been like absent a certain situation or specific event? Perhaps you would feel more normal. Maybe you would look back at the past without shame, regret, or anger.

Even if you have moved on with your life, you may find yourself wishing things had been different and wondering why God didn't stop what happened to you long ago. If He had, you think your life wouldn't be so hard. Maybe you wouldn't have a temper, feel anxious, hide, or live in a constant state of depression. Maybe you wouldn't feel like everyone else is happily living life just fine while you're struggling to keep up. Hello, Instagram and Facebook!

Here's another thought: What if what happened to you was actually part of God's plan of redemption? What Satan meant for evil, God meant for good. The very thorn in your flesh could be the catalyst for someone else's encouragement or even salvation (2 Cor. 12:7–10).

At one time I didn't understand why God allowed a horrific amount of suffering in my life. I have a better understanding today because of the work of the Holy Spirit. Jesus once told Peter something similar: "You do not realize now what I am doing, but later you will understand" (John 13:7).

Introduction

I used to think being a Christian would spare me from suffering. However, I have learned that being a Christian doesn't exempt you from pain, nor does being a Christian make you emotionally healthy. We all have to go through the process of sanctification (trials).

But my suffering is what paved the way for me to be able to talk about God's redemptive hand. Without my experiences, I would not understand how you feel. I would not be able to offer the same kind of encouragement (2 Cor. 1).

By no means am I a perfect soldier in this war, but I hope my battle scars can teach you something. Maybe my story can help you begin to have a conversation with your spouse. Perhaps my words could help you avoid some land mines along the way—or even a divorce.

While this book is about marriage, it is also about so much more. Because long before you married, there were likely lies you believed, hurts you accumulated, and shame you bore that you thought no one would ever know about. Sadly, your spouse may have opened up those old wounds without even knowing it. Now you are looking around at the collateral damage, wondering what happened.

My husband, Andy, and I went through a very tough season, and we, too, wondered what happened to us. Our marriage was interrupted by a lot of hard things at one time. It was the perfect storm. It felt like God gave us more than we could handle. Actually, He did, which is why we had no choice but to turn to Him. In fact, my counselor (who had worked at Minirth

INTRODUCTION

Meier clinics for 25 years) said my family's story was one of the top three most difficult family situations he had heard of in his time as a counselor. So, I understand suffering. But I also understand what it feels like to be free and to have a great marriage. Hang on! It's worth it to do the work.

My prayer is that this book will help you identify the baggage you brought in from your family of origin, the lies you have believed about yourself, and how you might be playing into Satan's blueprint for disharmony. By the end of this book, I hope you realize your spouse is not the enemy. (Satan is the real enemy.) Most of all, I pray my words point you to Jesus Christ who can heal your broken heart through forgiveness, truth, and biblical steps to unity.

It doesn't matter if your relationship is hanging on by a thread or if you are looking for ways to enhance your relationship with your spouse. There is something helpful for everyone in this book. In fact, you may laugh, cry, and be convicted of some very real things when you read these words; it's okay. I have done the same many times. If God can enable a certified chicken (me) to face the worst fears and ugliest pain, you can do the same. So, let's do it together because we all have a marriage interrupted by something.

PART I
INTERRUPTED

CHAPTER 1

Love at First Bite

"Life's deepest meaning is not found in accomplishments, but in relationships."

—Gary Chapman,
The Five Love Languages:
How to Express Heartfelt Commitment to Your Mate

We had only been married a few months when the big one hit. It was our first major fight as a married couple. And let me tell you, it was a doozy. The conversation started out innocently but went south within a matter of minutes.

I remember it like yesterday. I was standing in the living room of our 600-square-foot condo looking at my husband, Andy, when I blurted out something related to parenting our future kids. I don't remember exactly what I said, but it had something to do with their health. I wasn't even pregnant at the time—only dreaming about our babies.

I was surprised by his reaction. Instead of joining in my daydream, he responded more forcefully than usual. He wanted to assert his authority. More importantly, he wanted to make sure I knew what was expected of me as a mother before I got any big ideas of my own. The next thing I knew, he was outlining the health protocols for our non-existent children.

One of his proclamations was that we were going to feed our future children cod liver oil. I bristled at that notion. It sounded like something from the Dark Ages. I was envisioning a wicked mother (with a black hat and a wart on her nose) chasing our sweet babies around the house, spoon in hand, cramming the putrid liquid down their throats.

I was not going to be that kind of mother. And more than that, I wasn't going to let him unilaterally decide how to raise our children.

The last thing I remember about that conversation was Andy pointing his finger in my face and saying, "You will feed our children cod liver oil." That's when I lost my sanity and bit him.

I grabbed his finger, bit the fire out of it, and then ran to our bedroom, which was only about six feet from the living room. I slammed the door and locked it. I clearly remember that part. I don't actually remember biting him, but I do remember feeling devastated. Once I was in our bedroom, I fell into a puddle of tears on the bed, crying hysterically. What had I done? Who was this man I married? Regret filled my heart.

I had it so good as a single woman. I was poor as a church mouse living on a teacher's salary, but at least I had complete control over my life. No one told me what to do or gave me orders about imaginary children.

In a fit of rage, I looked at my surroundings and thought to myself, "I gave up my independence for this? What was I thinking?" My former apartment, where I once lived alone, was bigger than the cracker box we resided in as a married couple. On top of that, the new place was old and smelled musty. So what if we had moved into the uppity party of town; it didn't seem worth it. How could I have been so stupid? He had never responded to me this way when we were dating. What had I missed?

Sadly, that day I thought I had made the most horrible mistake of my life marrying my husband. But there was no going back. Sooner or later, I was going to have to unlock the bedroom door and let Andy in.

Not just into the bedroom, but into my life.

Except I didn't understand my life. I was just as shocked as he was when I bit him. I was even more horrified when I saw the bite marks. I didn't realize it at the time, but his finger-pointing (inappropriate on its own) had triggered memories from childhood, leading me to overreact. I should have simply told him to put his finger down and not to do that again, but that felt physically and emotionally impossible.

When he pointed his finger at me, everything went black. I couldn't talk, think, or process the situation for what it was because I was bombarded with old hurts, all in a matter of seconds. As I stood in the living room next to my husband, I was reminded of several people shaking their fingers in my face when I was younger.

I hated it every time it happened. I felt threatened, inferior, and powerless. And after many years of it happening repeatedly, I eventually felt rage. Even though those experiences happened years before, my husband's actions brought them to the forefront of my mind. It felt like a time warp; all those memories were compressed into the present.

Within seconds, the child inside of me realized she was big and had the power to rectify the situation; it was my day of reckoning. Unfortunately, when I bit Andy, I was "getting even" with the wrong person at the wrong time and using the wrong response. It didn't matter that my husband had never pointed his finger at me before. Someone was going to pay, and that day, it was Andy. Sadly, he was the recipient of all the venom I had stored up from years before.

I hate to admit this part—it felt good releasing all my rage on him, although I knew it was wrong. I felt like a pressure cooker that had built up steam for years and finally blew. It should have been a red flag. I had no idea what was smoldering inside of me.

Fortunately, Andy did learn that day not to shake his finger at me ever again. And he has never done it since; I made my point. But I knew there had to be a better way to resolve conflict between us. After all, I couldn't bite him every time we had a problem.

After that incident, I tried hard to watch my behavior. However, another situation later the same month further exposed my wounds from the past. We were going over the checkbook together. Andy, who is an accountant, liked to regularly keep up with the expenditures, which was reasonable. When we got to the grocery store bill, he paused, made an ugly face, and then proceeded to ask me why I spent so much money. (He definitely needed help with delivery.)

After five minutes of rationalizing my purchases, I felt furious. How dare he question my grocery choices or make such an ugly face at me. Instead of telling him how I felt, I threw the checkbook at him and again broke down in tears. I told him I was never going over finances with him again. To an accountant, that's like declaring war.

Shutting down was my way of protecting myself from outside threats. Clearly, my husband was now an outside threat that had invaded my space. He had unintentionally dredged up other memories.

First I bit him, and then I was throwing things. What was wrong with me? Why was I so triggered by his behavior? I had never done this before. In a span of one month, I had let my guard down twice. I felt exposed. The man I deeply loved had poked some very raw places. I was incredibly embarrassed.

I also felt shame. Andy was starting to see who I really was—an insecure woman, scared of abandonment and afraid of rejection. I felt like a wounded animal when questioned, challenged, or pushed. In turn, I lashed out in odd ways that were shocking even to me. What I really wanted was for him to hold me and tell me everything was going to be okay. To tell the little girl inside of me, who was desperately looking for unconditional love, that she was going to be okay. But I didn't know how to ask for this, and he didn't know how to comfort me or approach me in a softer way.

The reality was that our marriage exposed both of our vulnerabilities in ways we never thought possible. That day, I resolved to never let my husband see that wounded girl again.

Burying my emotions was the only way I had learned to deal with conflict while growing up, so that is what I did in marriage.

It was a survival mechanism that had always worked in the past. Why would I change it now?

I just needed to do a better job of hiding my feelings so even my husband wouldn't know what simmered below the surface. Truthfully, I didn't want to know what was below the surface either. The whole idea of digging deeper into my feelings scared me. Frankly, I was afraid if I opened all the wounds I would never recover.

I told myself I was fine. Denial was safe. I didn't need to unearth things that were better left alone. I had no idea I was ill-equipped to deal with problems in a healthy way, nor did I know how to appropriately express my feelings to my husband when I was hurting.

They don't teach these things in school. Instead, we tend to do what was modeled for us growing up. But let me assure you that my parents didn't bite. We also don't possess conflict resolution skills by sheer instinct. They have to be learned. By default, instinct usually leads to pride and unforgiveness. But it doesn't have to be this way.

Perhaps like me so many years ago, you don't know exactly what is wrong in your marriage, but you know something is "off" because you are shocked by your own behaviors or the behaviors of your spouse. Rest assured, there is hope.

In Part I of this book, I peel back the curtain on our early marriage issues and discuss some of the typical problems you may be facing as a couple—job and money stress, health issues, and difficult family relationships, to name a few. While you may not identify with every problem we faced, you may see yourself in the ways we behaved toward each other during conflict. And that is the real goal—to open your eyes to how you treat your spouse.

In Part II of this book, I give biblical wisdom to not only help you have a healthy marriage, but also work on yourself. You are half of the equation, whether or not you believe it. (Yes, I was shocked too when I figured this out.) Included is an awesome story of redemption at the end. It's so incredible that only God can get the glory.

My prayer for you is that you not only learn from our marriage successes, but also our mistakes (and laugh at a few of them). One of my biggest mistakes was stuffing my feelings internally. I then moved to a more covert way of handling our problems—revenge.

REFLECTION

1. How do you deal with conflict?

2. What old wounds are contributing to unhealthy response tendencies with your spouse?

3. What subjects are off-limits because they are too painful to discuss? Or because they trigger heated discussions?

4. How are you listening to your spouse and hearing his or her hurts? Do you understand what he or she really needs from you?

5. What deep fissures are you ignoring in your relationship?

CHAPTER REVIEW

1. When we don't know how to deal with conflict appropriately, we use tools we learned from childhood.

2. Some of the coping tools used as a child worked okay then, but they don't work well as an adult.

3. Your spouse may be shocked by your reaction, not realizing he or she triggered something in your past.

4. You can change the trajectory of your marriage, but it starts with you.

VERSE FOR SPIRITUAL WARFARE

Proverbs 15:18

*"A hot-tempered person stirs up a conflict,
but the one who is patient calms a quarrel."*

PRAYER

God, I come to You now, and I give You our marriage. I ask that You take our brokenness and make us new. I realize we do not have the capability to do this on our own without Your Holy Spirit. We need You to step in right now and help us change in ways we never thought possible.

I ask You to help both of us put down our pride and self-protective tendencies so we can truly identify the issues we are encountering on a daily basis. Show us individually how to be more like You, even though our flesh cries out to do the opposite. I lay down the expectations I have for my spouse and ask You to fulfill my needs with the portion You have allotted me. I realize my spouse will never be able to meet all of my needs like You do. I release this, right now. Clothe us with compassion, kindness, humility, gentleness, and patience as we move forward.

CHAPTER 2

The Revenge Muffins

"Man must evolve for all human conflict a method which rejects revenge, aggression and retaliation. The foundation of such a method is love."

—Martin Luther King, Jr.,
Acceptance Speech for the Nobel Peace Prize

It was a Sunday morning, and we were running late for church. I had volunteered to bring muffins for our Sunday school class but failed to tell Andy about it until an hour and half before church started.

As usual, I had slept in. Getting up early was not my strong suit. (Still isn't.) I already had a bad habit of being late for church, and the muffins just complicated the matter. I thought perhaps Andy would help me that morning since I was running behind, but I guessed wrong.

I was making blueberry muffins; however, they were nothing like his mother's wheat germ muffins from scratch. Mine came from a box. Andy was not only horrified that I was using a box mix, but he was also sure I was going to poison our Sunday school class with the junkified version that included white flour and white sugar.

I was on my own that day. My muffins and I had both been rejected in one fell swoop. Resentfully, I made breakfast, baked the muffins, and tried to get dressed in the remaining 20 minutes before Sunday school started.

Meanwhile, Andy went on a jog, casually ate his breakfast, and leisurely dressed for church. And then he angrily waited for me until I was ready to leave.

I didn't talk to him the whole morning—mostly because I was running around like a crazy woman, but also because I was furious that he was not at all engaged in my emergency. I thought he would eventually show some sort of empathy. Nope.

I slammed the pans around, grunted, sighed, and rolled my eyes at him, hoping he would help me. He didn't take the bait. He was going to take a stand that morning; it was a crime to cook unhealthy muffins in our kitchen, and it was a crime to be late.

I was going to pay.

When we finally got in the car, we immediately started to argue. We were late for church again, and this time people were counting on us for food. We continued to bicker throughout the 15-minute drive, but when we got out of the car, the show began. As soon as we slammed the car doors, we both put on the "happy act." (I am sure this has never happened to you on a Sunday morning.) Both Andy and I smiled, greeted our friends in the hallway at church, and then entered our classroom like a typical newlywed couple in love. No one was the wiser.

The Revenge Muffins

We quickly apologized for being late, and everyone helped themselves to the muffins. Thankfully, it turned out to be no big deal. Only I noticed that my husband refused to eat one of the junky muffins I baked. This added more fuel to the fire.

After Sunday school, I went to get my plate of muffins. There were still a few left over, so I wrapped them up to take home. We walked to the church service without talking. Well, I talked to everyone else but him. The silent treatment was in full force.

During church, we sang, prayed, listened to the sermon, and sang again at the benediction. After visiting with friends, we left. Once in the car, we went back to our old selves. We continued in silence all the way home.

Nothing that was taught in Sunday school or in the pastor's sermon that day had penetrated our hearts. The last few hours had been a waste of time.

Back at our condo, Andy got out of the car and went inside without ever looking back. Still sitting in the car, I looked out the windshield as he slipped behind the door. I wondered what happened. How could we have gotten so far off track in just a few short months of marriage? Slowly, I gathered my purse, Bible, and the plate of muffins, but my mind was racing—what was I going to do next?

As I struggled to get the car door open with all my belongings in hand, I noticed the muffins were precariously balanced. I half-heartedly secured them, thinking I only had to make it a few yards. When I got to the building, I tried to pull the old door open; it was stuck. After another yank, I managed to nudge it open and slip in the door. But as I walked down the hallway, I lost control of the plate. The muffins flew in front of me and bounced down the hallway.

As I stared at those muffins, I hoped for some inspiration, as if they could talk back to me and tell me what to do next. I felt defeated. Even the muffins were giving me the "silent treatment."

I picked up the dirty muffins and noticed they faintly smelled of bug spray. Yuck. There was no way I was going to eat them. Embarrassed by my lack of agility, I put them back on the plate and walked into our condo. I went into the kitchen and set them down by the sink so I could dispose of them, only I got distracted.

Ruminating about the morning, I went to put up the rest of my belongings. I thought, "If only I had not dropped the last three muffins, I could have eaten them in front of Andy and showed him who was boss." I was not going to be told how or what to cook in my kitchen.

A minute later I looked up and noticed Andy had grabbed one of the dirty muffins. He asked, "Do you mind if I have one?" He was trying to make peace. I briefly thought about telling him they rolled down the dirty hallway, but I was so angry with him that I continued in silence. No part of me was feeling charitable that day. He had gone too far, and the time for peace was long gone.

I wanted revenge.

I planned to die on this hill. So, I shrugged at him; it would be my private joke. He would never know where they had just been. To seal the deal I said, "No. Eat all you want."

The Revenge Muffins

After he ate the whole thing, I couldn't contain myself. Slowly, I started laughing. Eventually, I was doubled over, laughing hysterically. I felt a bit guilty, but mostly, I was giddy with pure joy. I could not have planned it any better. It was almost too good to be true.

I felt completely vindicated. The only problem was Andy wasn't in on the joke. And he definitely didn't know the joke was on him. So, I proceeded to tell him every gory detail about how the muffins rolled down the hall on the nasty carpet. And that there were probably enough germs on the contaminated muffins to kill a dinosaur. I'm sure I exaggerated a bit just to aggravate him even more.

One look at Andy's face and you would have thought I deliberately poisoned him. He turned white, started gagging, and took deep breaths to keep from choking. (Remember, he's a health food nut.) Immediately, he leaned over the sink trying to spit out any remnants of the contaminated muffin. He was wiping his tongue, making horrible faces in disgust, all the while gasping for air. Andy was so fastidious about what went into his body that the thought of 30 years of foot traffic, pet poo, and bug spray was too much for him to handle.

For a moment, I thought he was really getting sick but soon realized he was just having a meltdown. The more he spat, hissed, and wiped his tongue, the harder I laughed. Seriously, I could not stop laughing. I didn't really want him to get sick. I just wanted him to think he might get sick. I wanted him to think about the nasty carpet for a good long while.

After a few minutes, Andy calmed down and realized he was going to be okay. Soon enough, he thought it was funny too. It broke the ice between us and helped us to start a conversation. A whole lot had gone wrong that morning. We each had some things that needed changing.

Laughter does that. It opens our hearts and helps us to receive something that would otherwise not penetrate our stubborn wills. Even though I enjoyed every bite he took of that muffin, down deep I knew my tactics were not healthy. Seeking revenge, employing the silent treatment, and burying my emotions had not worked. They were childish in nature.

So, what did work? I couldn't figure out the magic words to navigate conflict in a healthy way. I didn't know how to show up as an adult and have an adult conversation.

Perhaps, like I was, you are looking for that epic moment in your life when your spouse comes to you with great sorrow and remorse because you said just the right thing to penetrate the heart. You have it all planned out. He or she will grovel for a while and ask for forgiveness until you feel completely vindicated. Only then will you offer grace. Until then, you plan on punishing with cutting remarks, contempt, silence, or even dirty muffins.

What you may not realize is that when we are bitter and can't let go, we deceive ourselves into thinking revenge will help us feel better and clear the slate. But the slate is never clear, no matter what the other person does. It will never be enough.

The Revenge Muffins

Revenge will never even the score or help recoup what you have lost. Instead, it escalates the problem to a new level. Sin heaped on sin doesn't negate sin, nor does it erase the problems.

Truthfully, I wanted to be a good wife, and Andy wanted to be a good husband. We wanted our marriage to succeed, like most couples do in the beginning, but the childish coping skills we used to deal with conflict were sabotaging us as adults. And when it came to healthy behavior, we just didn't have all the tools needed to fight fairly and resolve our differences. We needed to go back to the beginning and retrace our steps.

REFLECTION

1. Are you angry at your spouse? Even bitter?

2. How might you overreact when offenses happen?

3. In what ways do you revert to childish tactics (silent treatment, pouting, yelling, seeking revenge, etc.) when you are hurt or don't get your way?

4. Do you think revenge will help you grow stronger as a couple? Will it help you grow closer to God?

5. What are some healthier behaviors you can practice next time you have conflict?

CHAPTER REVIEW

1. Revenge will never even the score or help recoup what you have lost.

2. Revenge is destructive in marriage. Sin heaped on sin doesn't negate sin.

3. Talking things through is much better than seeking revenge.

4. Forgiveness and grace should be extended because God forgave us first.

VERSES FOR SPIRITUAL WARFARE

1 Peter 3:9

"Do not repay evil with evil or insult with insult. On the contrary, repay evil with blessing, because to this you were called so that you may inherit a blessing."

Proverbs 20:22

"Do not say, 'I'll pay you back for this wrong!' Wait for the LORD and he will avenge you."

PRAYER

God, help me to love my spouse the way You love us. As much as my flesh wants revenge, penetrate my heart and show me how to forgive even the worst offenses done to me. Let us have the courage to honestly address difficult situations in a healthy manner without adding sin to an already difficult situation.

Let Your Holy Spirit convict us both where we are not aligned with Your word. I pray for blessings instead of curses on my spouse's life. I ask You to restore the love we may have lost for each other in the chaos. Help me to wait on You instead of trying to fix him/her myself. Only You can heal my spouse's heart from the inside out. Thank You, God, that You are transforming us to be the husband and wife You called us to be according to the scriptures.

CHAPTER 3

Hard Endings Are Just Beginings

"All endings are also beginnings. We just don't know it at the time."

—Mitch Albom,
The Five People You Meet in Heaven

I grew up as a PK (preacher's kid). Well, kind of. There are some interesting years in my family history. My parents were actually millionaires before they became Christians. At 23, my father owned a restaurant called The Italian Village and a nightclub called Gringos, both housed in the same building.

Gringos was the first nightclub in Texas and an automatic success the first week it opened. Not only did the Dallas elite come through their doors, but also those visiting from Hollywood and Las Vegas. Both of my parents had a lot of responsibilities (and a lot of fun) at a young age. I realize this is not the usual résumé for a pastor, but there is nothing usual about my family.

My dad is a full-blooded Italian. Sicilian. He is an amazing chef and can repair just about anything. My mom is a beautiful strawberry blonde and is part Norwegian. She was a knockout. They married when they were just barely 20. There were a lot of "sparks" in their relationship, and unfortunately the dynamic was sometimes unstable. By the time my parents hit their 30s, they were headed for divorce.

My dad was angry and disillusioned with all his success. He had made it to the top and found the proverbial man with the levers behind the curtain. Oz was not all it was cracked up to be. There was nothing there in the Emerald City but more stress, bigger bills, betrayal, and constant fighting at home.

My father cried out to God in desperation because he was empty. Several weeks after that prayer, he was filming a commercial at a local television station. The station had just converted to Christian programming. It was there he found Jesus, through an amazing series of events.

That one decision was so polarizing that it made local and national headlines, primarily because he then refused to serve alcohol in his establishment. Not many understood his subsequent business decisions, but my father walked away from all that money and notoriety. Some thought he had literally gone crazy.

My mom didn't understand either, but she stood by him. Eventually, she was introduced to Jesus, and it all made sense to her as well. Truthfully, I believe if God had not intervened during those years, my parents would have divorced.

However, not everyone in this miraculous story was happy. My grandparents, who started the restaurant in the 1940s, were furious when my dad accepted Christ. They felt what my dad had done to the family business was unforgivable. They had been publicly humiliated on a national level.

Hard Endings Are Just Beginnings

After many heated discussions, they disowned us. (Yes, some Italians really do disown their families.) The relationship with my grandparents never mended. Consequently, I never knew my paternal grandparents. And I didn't just lose them when our family split. I also lost aunts, uncles, cousins, and other relatives.

Somewhere amidst all the turmoil our cook and housekeeper left too. I was deeply attached to many of these people, especially the ones who took care of me on a regular basis.

My parents were devastated. Unfortunately, they couldn't help my sisters or me make sense of it all. Truthfully, they didn't understand what happened either. It seemed God was asking my parents to give up everything and make a complete life change. In hindsight, it was a good thing.

But at the time, all I knew was that a bunch of people I cared about had left me. I couldn't figure out what I had done wrong. So many people had disappeared from my life in such a short time. Was I that bad of a kid?

I thought if I were cute enough, sweet enough, or smart enough they would come back. Sadly, that didn't happen. It was a cruel reality that left a hole in my heart. That's when I started telling myself I wasn't enough. In fact, I thought it was my fault that my grandparents disowned us. It was too much for me to process at the young age of seven.

After that devastating loss, I internalized the idea that people leave. I didn't know why. I just felt that if I didn't live up to expectations, it could happen again at any time. To make things more confusing, the expectations in my family elevated as I grew older. Our family was long on rules and short on grace. Nothing less than perfection was acceptable. It was confusing as a growing Christian.

In one sense, the estrangement from my grandparents created a generational stronghold that set a horrible precedent. However, looking back, I realize my grandparents were not healthy people in any way. Being away from them was probably the safest thing at the time for all of us. Unfortunately, it took decades to unravel our family history and see the truth.

My parents were caught up in their own hurts, just as I was. It wasn't until years later that I learned to step back and see the whole picture through a lens of forgiveness. Only then did I see the deep hurts my parents carried. My heart broke when I realized they both had their own tragedies that plagued them. That dark history of our family legacy was a huge part of it.

As a Christian, I had a hard time explaining our family split. The normal platitudes didn't apply to our situation. My mind was trying to balance two different realities: Christians don't endorse family splits, but my family had a dark history no one truly understood. Really dark. How do you explain this to people without getting into the gory details? Mostly you can't, so you just have to risk being judged and misunderstood.

After the family split, my dad kept the Italian restaurant open and turned the club into a Christian entertainment venue. All the big names in Christian music played there. It did okay for several years. Eventually, it closed.

The glory days were over. The money stopped coming in when they stopped serving alcohol. My parents were no longer the popular kids with the "it" factor. In fact, to the outside world, it looked like they had self-imploded. Furthermore, my father had no job prospects when he handed the keys back to his estranged father, my grandfather.

It takes maturity and a long perspective to see that sometimes hard endings are just the beginning of something new. After the restaurant closed, the only job my dad could find was at our local church. He became the maintenance man. It was a big fall from the top. After a year in that role, my father moved up to business administrator. When I was in seventh grade, he became the associate pastor, and soon after, our little Baptist church became a megachurch.

When I was in 11th grade, my father and another pastor decided to start a new church in Dallas, Texas. It, too, became a megachurch. This is where I met my husband, Andy. Thank goodness for hard endings and new beginnings.

I remember that Wednesday evening. About 20 teenagers had gathered for youth group in a friend's game room. After we sat down, the youth director asked us to go around the room and introduce ourselves. When it got to Andy, he gave his name and age, and he told a little bit about himself. I immediately perked up when I saw this handsome, blonde boy who just happened to be in my grade.

My friend must have read my mind because she nudged me hard and said loudly, "Hey, he's cute." To my chagrin, every person in the room heard her. Suddenly, it got quiet, and everyone started laughing. They all stared at me like I had a piece of spinach between my teeth. I wanted to crawl under the couch and hide. Andy smiled at me, and then we both looked away in embarrassment. After that incident, I shied away from him for months. As fate would have it, though, we finally did become friends.

The following summer, I asked my parents if I could change schools for my senior year because I wasn't learning much where I attended. Without hesitating, my parents agreed to look for a better learning environment. We chose a school closer to my home, and I enrolled in August. On the first day of school, I was told to go to the sanctuary for chapel. When I walked into the sanctuary, I felt overwhelmed.

After scanning the crowd, I met eyes with Andy. I had no idea he went to the same school. We were both shocked but pleasantly surprised. Over the next few weeks, he helped me transition to my new environment. By October, we were dating. I was madly in love with him. I think he felt the same way about me too.

For the next eight years, we weaved in and out of each other's lives. When we were 25, we decided to get married. We had loved each other for years. Like any good bride-to-be, I suggested we go to pre-marital counseling before we married. With the confidence of a young, red-blooded male, Andy said we didn't need it. After all, what was there to talk about? We had dated off and on for eight years.

I, on the other hand, thought we needed to discuss how our marriage was going to work. I was especially worried about how we were going to handle money. I kept pushing, but Andy wasn't interested. He said we knew everything already; it was a waste of time. I finally gave up asking.

Soon after we married, I realized there were fissures in the foundation. While Andy was a wonderful husband, we needed some help learning how to resolve conflict (the biting incident was the first clue). But a couple of months later, I became pregnant with our first child. And that was that. We were too distracted with a baby, remodeling, work, church, family, etc. There was no time to examine any underlying cracks, much less address them.

In their book *Vertical Marriage*, Dave and Ann Wilson wisely state:

> Contrary to popular belief, ignoring conflict doesn't make it go away; it makes it worse. Ignoring conflict is akin to turning up your car radio so you won't hear that annoying grinding noise coming from your engine. Give it a few miles, and the noise will be the least of your problems. Here is an immutable truth concerning relationships: When it comes to conflict, nothing is worse than doing nothing. (page 112)

Sadly, we had not yet come to realize this. And the conflict resolution tools we carried into marriage were marginal at best. My tendency was to run away, hide, and quietly ruminate about any injustices, wallowing in self-pity. Sometimes I would turn to revenge, if all else failed. Muffins, anyone?

Andy's approach to problems was just to suck it up and push through. Or ignore it and hope it would go away. We were both naturally pulled in opposite directions due to our temperaments. So much that we couldn't step back and see what was happening.

Unfortunately, it took three very difficult problems colliding at one time to get our attention and prompt us to change our ways. Any one of these difficulties would have been enough for a couple, but three major problems at once felt like too much. It was too much.

God allowed Andy's job difficulties, my declining health, and a family estrangement—all of which affected our marriage—to show us that God loved us fully and completely in our brokenness.

Furthermore, He used these interruptions to move us out of our comfort zones. We thought the way we had been handling conflict was normal. It wasn't until we were overwhelmed with our hurts that we were finally willing to address and change our sinful patterns.

I was just trying to be a good wife and mother, and Andy was trying to be a good husband, father, and provide for his family. While these things seemed honorable at the time, God required more from us as a married couple than we realized.

REFLECTION

1. What is your family history? Write down major events in your life.

2. What traumatic events from years ago are affecting your marriage now?

3. Ask your spouse to articulate how you handle conflict. Does it match what you thought?

4. Will you commit right now to change the way you handle conflict with your spouse, if it is unhealthy?

5. What steps will you take to change your behaviors?

CHAPTER REVIEW

1. Taking time to look back at your family history will help you understand why you behave the way you do now.

2. Addressing unhealthy conflict resolution tendencies will help you stay united as a couple.

3. Choosing to continue in your unhealthy behavior patterns will not only eat at your marriage but may also destroy it.

VERSES FOR SPIRITUAL WARFARE

James 1:19–20

"My dear brothers and sisters, take note of this: Everyone should be quick to listen, slow to speak and slow to become angry, because human anger does not produce the righteousness that God desires."

Proverbs 15:1

"A gentle answer turns away wrath, but a harsh word stirs up anger."

PRAYER

God, I thank You that You knit me in my mother's womb many years ago. I was planned by You even before You breathed life into man. I was not a mistake, nor was the family You placed me in when I was born. I know there is no perfect family, so I ask You to help me forgive hurts that are still lingering from the past.

Help me to release any family members who may have intentionally or unintentionally hurt me while growing up. Bind my wounds and heal my broken heart and the heart of my spouse. I know we pass a spiritual inheritance down to the next generation, so let ours be a godly one that is both peaceful and unified.

CHAPTER 4
A Job Well Done

"Change is painful. Few people have the courage to seek out change. Most people won't change until the pain of where they are exceeds the pain of change."

—Dave Ramsey,
The Total Money Makeover

When most couples get married, there is an overwhelming pressure to achieve the American dream: a decent job, a home, two cars, and money left over for vacations.

We were no different.

Since there were no great-uncles or distant relatives who had left us large sums of money, we were trapped in the same rat race as most every other married couple. To make matters worse, the job Andy had at the time helped create our perfect storm. It was so demanding that it continuously encroached on our personal time.

He would often get emergency phone calls during dinners, weekends, holidays, and even vacations. The ever-present crisis couldn't wait until the next day or the next week to get resolved. Often we would be out spending time together or doing something fun with the kids and the phone would ring.

By the way Andy contorted his face, I could tell it was the office calling again.

Then off he would go.

Andy would move to a quiet corner or disappear into another room for 30 minutes or longer, only to magically return to the scene as quickly as he left, nonchalantly trying to reengage with the family and catch up on what he missed.

Unfortunately, that didn't always work out so well. He may have been present in body, but his mind was off somewhere else solving the latest financial emergency. Don't get me wrong—I was proud of him. He was well-respected for his financial acumen at a young age, but I resented the fact that his boss got more time with him than I did. And he robbed me of the time we did have together as a couple. I hated sharing him.

Andy was trapped in a very difficult situation that had no real solutions. I truly felt bad for him. I clearly understood that he was caught between work and home. Often work won because it paid the bills, so I didn't complain too much. Nevertheless, I heard that quiet voice whispering lies, telling me he would rather be at work than at home with me and the kids.

An encroaching boss wasn't all that plagued us in our early married years. What to do with the money once it was in the bank account was a whole other discussion. In a marriage there is usually a spender and a saver. But if you are married to an accountant, that automatically makes you the spender and somewhat "suspect" by default.

Since Andy was a CPA (Certified Public Accountant), he thought it would be a good thing for me to learn some sort of software that would help us track our money. At first, I balked. Why should I learn how to track all the money? That was his job! He was the accountant.

After Andy pushed for months, I finally sat down and slowly learned how to navigate the finance-management software.

I hated it.

I thought it was one of the dumbest things ever created. For me, putting numbers in boxes was akin to nails scratching on a chalkboard, a root canal, or listening to a baby scream in an airplane for five hours. As an added bonus, Andy thought it would be fun if we broke down all of our groceries into categories.

Oh, yay. More work. Like a good wife, I complied (with a bad attitude).

You may wonder if it is possible to know how much money a person can spend on dairy, snacks, meat, vegetables, toiletries, and "other" in one month. I am here to tell you it is possible. I got an official monthly report. But, in my mind, it was an assessment of how bad a person I had been that particular month. I took everything as a personal assault since I did most of the spending.

As you can imagine, this created a lot of resentment. So what if we knew how much I spent at the grocery store, including the "other" category. We needed to eat! It meant nothing to me other than my husband had gone bonkers.

This further aggravated the situation.

Tracking the groceries by category was definitely overkill, but Andy just wanted to know what we were spending every month. I, on the other hand, felt criticized even though I was doing everything he asked. Each month it felt like I came up short.

When I scoffed at the numbers, Andy felt I didn't appreciate what it took to make a living. He didn't think I understood the sacrifices he made for our family. He thought I wasn't being a team player. Many times, we would get into a "discussion" after reviewing the report, and then I would end up angry or crying. (In the early days before the computer, I would simply throw the checkbook, as I mentioned in the first chapter.)

I knew he handled other people's money for a living. But this was different because it was my money too. He wanted to do it his way, and I wanted to do it my way. Sound familiar?

Neither of us fully trusted the other when it came to our finances, which made it next to impossible to sit down and hash out a reasonable budget that included a give-and-take from both sides. As Christians, we knew we needed to tithe. But we didn't know how much. Gross or net? Additionally, neither of us knew how to put what we needed and wanted into words without setting the other person off.

These arguments about our "aggressive" accounting system just indicated a bigger problem: We didn't know how to talk to each other about his job, our spending, or our saving. We were clueless to what was really going on. For my part, a fear of abandonment, control, and the lies I believed about myself were coming into play. Andy also didn't realize he had his own hurts from his family of origin that were complicating our discussions.

A Job Well Done

Perhaps you, too, have issues with your job, or maybe you struggle to manage your money as a team. Instead of being a unified front, you are pitted against each other, demanding your needs are met without considering the whole picture. Maybe you are scared to have that hard conversation because you know it won't end well. I understand.

After years of dealing with conflict like this, something had to give. We were both comfortably set in a pattern that needed to be interrupted. That's when all hell descended on our marriage. That next season of suffering was so intense we just held on for dear life. I wanted to run away and disappear. In a way, that's just what I did.

REFLECTION

1. Is your job or your spouse's job causing problems in your marriage? If so, do you feel unheard, controlled, or unappreciated?

2. How are money issues from your family of origin causing added stress to your financial situation now? Do you trust each other?

3. Are you both honest about what you are spending? And saving?

4. In what ways will you show up as two healthy adults and put together a realistic budget?

5. Is your tithe the most important line item in your budget?

CHAPTER REVIEW

1. It is important to get on the same page financially. If you are not having regular conversations about money, now is the time to start talking.
2. Family of origin issues surrounding money may be playing into your conversations. Look at your behavior to see how you react.

A JOB WELL DONE

VERSE FOR SPIRITUAL WARFARE

Proverbs 15:16

*"Better a little with the fear of the L*ORD
than great wealth with turmoil."

PRAYER

God, I give our finances to You. I thank You for what You have already provided for us. Help us willingly give over any area we have not completely surrendered. Keep us from freely spending without accountability. Show us how to work together so we are not oppressed by debt. Give us wisdom to plan for our future.

I ask You to show us creative ways to steward our money so it will go further. Help us to be generous to others in need. I pray greed will not be a part of our legacy. I ask for Your hand of protection over our finances—that our resources will not be devoured by the evil one. Don't let either one of us give into anxiety, but instead help us to trust You to provide for us in ways we can't even imagine. Give us wisdom to know the right direction for each of our careers. If one of us chooses to stay home with kids, I pray You will help us trust You in this decision.

CHAPTER 5

The Disappearing Act

"Invisible tears are the hardest to wipe away."

—Author Unknown

Right after the birth of our second child, I started having digestive problems. I had been dealing with stomach issues before then, but it had been manageable. This was different. The cramping and bloating became unbearable. Many times, I found myself up all night in severe pain, only to be relieved the next day after the food passed through my digestive tract.

After several trips to the emergency room, the doctors said they couldn't find anything wrong and diagnosed it as IBS (Irritable Bowel Syndrome). I learned that's what they say when they don't know what is wrong.

I remember laughing to myself when I heard the diagnosis. Basically, I was irritated, which couldn't have been more accurate. I felt that way about everyone, including my husband. I was trying so hard to be a good wife, mother, and daughter. But it was never enough, in my mind. Meanwhile, I was feeling more and more invisible to those around me. I felt like if I voiced my opinion I was always rebuffed. Mentally, I could not handle anyone disliking me or disapproving of me.

I was a hard-core people-pleaser. In fact, many times I felt wrong for having feelings or an opinion at all. I kept telling myself I was stupid, too emotional, and always the one at fault. Eventually, I shut down and stopped trying to tell those around me how I felt. It caused too much conflict.

I thought if I could jump through the right hoops, everyone would approve of me and love me. I was afraid of being unloved. I was afraid of being abandoned. Andy never said anything specific to make me think this; it was a lie I perpetuated myself, stemming from the past.

I managed this cycle of people-pleasing for several more years, but at the same time, my physical symptoms increased in frequency and severity. I found myself at the hospital having a colonoscopy on our seventh wedding anniversary. What a way to celebrate!

That day I was diagnosed with a real disease. At the time, the doctor called it proctitis—a form of ulcerative colitis. It only affected the lower portion of my colon. The doctor sent me home with several prescriptions and said there was nothing else he could do. Naively, I thought if I took the medicine everything would be fine. However, that was not the case. But I was able to manage the flareups for another eight years.

During that time, Andy and I became increasingly more agitated with each other. He was unhappy at his job, and I was unhappy with the number of hours he was working and away from our family. There were days I felt like he looked at me as more of a liability than an asset due to my illness. He didn't understand why I couldn't just get my act together and

The Disappearing Act

do what I was supposed to do. Frankly, I was wondering the same thing.

My physical distress eventually led to greater emotional distress. Depression put its hooks in me and wouldn't let go. All the while, those themes of rejection and abandonment from childhood kept resounding in my mind. Sadly, I had no idea they were so wrong or destructive; it was just the program that normally played in my brain. A sick recording.

It didn't matter that I had been a Christian for many years. The thoughts in my head were louder than what the Bible said about me. Quietly, God kept whispering in my ear: loved, accepted, forgiven, important, beloved, redeemed. Only I didn't believe it. The lies were hardwired. My "truth," not God's truth, was what caused the unhealthy behaviors toward others and toward myself. Frankly, I didn't know what to believe. Or who I was. I was just an extension of everyone else. I had lost myself.

In fact, I self-destructed for no good reason.

Reality sunk in the day I stood on the scale, and it said 100 pounds (I am 5'8"). It was hard to look at myself in the mirror. I had lost 30 pounds in three short months. I was slowly disappearing, which is what I subconsciously wanted to do.

Everything I ate came right back out. I couldn't even drink water without ill effects. The symptoms had become unbearable. After eight days of not eating, I called the doctor. He immediately ordered a colonoscopy to see what was wrong. I was sure it was cancer. I knew it was bad.

The next day my sister, not Andy, took me to the hospital. Andy had a demanding job with an enormous workload that left him very little time for anything else. On top of that, he was worried about how we were going to pay for all the medical bills we were accumulating. It was too much for him, so he stayed disengaged from the whole situation.

I felt like an utter disappointment and a huge bother to my husband. We had both settled into basically separate lives, each of us trying to just survive. Truthfully, I wanted Andy to go with me to the procedure, but I was too afraid to ask him. I couldn't handle the rejection if he said no. I knew if I forced him, he would be resentful. And that would be worse than hearing "no." Then I would know for sure that he didn't love me or want to be with me.

After the colonoscopy, I lay in bed in the cold room waiting for the doctor to return. Secretly, I hoped I wouldn't wake up from the procedure. I was tired.

Tired of trying to be perfect, tired of not being enough, tired of living this brand of Christianity that included porous boundaries and no identity of my own.

Fortunately, I did come through the procedure just fine, but what I heard next was devastating. The nurse, not the doctor, came in and matter-of-factly said the words, "You have Crohn's disease."

She went on: "You are probably going to lose your colon and have a bag (ileostomy) for an intestine the rest of your life, since the disease has now migrated into your small intestine. The doctor is going to have to take out the lower portion of your colon. It looks like hamburger meat." And then she walked out.

The Disappearing Act

To her, it was as if she had told me the sky was blue. It was something so menial it was hardly worth mentioning. There was no emotion whatsoever in her voice. No words of hope or even the slightest sympathy for my new diagnosis. It was like she was disgusted with me too.

I felt angry, hopeless, and alone. In fact, I have never felt more alone than I did that day. More importantly, I felt God had left me. Or maybe He was never there in the first place. Perhaps Christianity was all just a ruse.

I seriously thought God loved everyone else, just not me. My illness seemed like a cruel joke. How could a loving God allow me to suffer in such horrendous pain? Every flareup was as intense as childbirth. And now this. I was going to be cut up like a car in a chop shop. My organs were going to be severed into pieces and thrown into the trash like garbage. Was I garbage too?

I was terrified. My future looked grim. I didn't want to have a bag attached to the side of my body for the rest of my life. The combination of the smell, the noises, and the utter shame was more than I could handle. I would never want to go in public again.

And what about my marriage? That was even more frightening. How was Andy going to handle the news? I knew my husband would never physically leave me over this, but because of my past issues with abandonment, I wasn't sure if he would withdraw in other ways. I would be embarrassed to be intimate with that kind of alteration to my body.

I had been so sick for the previous three months, I was positive I would not live another year. Frankly, I wasn't sure I wanted to live another year. As I was lying in bed that day in the hospital, I knew what was wrong with me. The denial left, and my eyes were opened. I could no longer run from the underlying problem. I was angry.

I wasn't just a little angry. I was filled with bitterness, hatred, even rage. It was a deep, dark feeling I could no longer control. The bitterness had been simmering in my heart for years. From the outside, it looked like I was okay. I had done an excellent job of hiding my feelings from everyone, including myself. In fact, I had purposely stuffed my feelings down deep into my soul just to keep functioning. But my body kept score. My body knew the truth, even when I didn't.

I was tired of living one way and feeling another. My habit of meeting everyone else's needs while neglecting my own was about to destroy me. I concluded I could no longer continue to jump through hoops to make everyone else happy.

Foolishly, I had thought pleasing everyone else was what it meant to be a good Christian. Instead, I felt empty, unvalidated, and worthless. In fact, I hated myself because I lacked the courage to set healthy boundaries with those around me. I was scared if I said "no" I would be abandoned again.

I didn't think I could take another person walking away from me if I didn't perform. Those lies were implanted early in my life and were wreaking havoc years later.

But after the Crohn's diagnosis, I no longer cared. Right there in the hospital bed, I decided to cut off my relationship with my parents. It was the logical choice at the time, due to many unresolved issues between us. My relationship with them was causing me the most stress by far. (Check out my book *Estranged: Finding Hope When Your Family Falls Apart* for more details.)

I didn't know how I would do it or how long it would take. That didn't matter to me. I just knew I had to leave my family to get well. Otherwise, I was going to lose my colon. I didn't care if I had to run to Mexico, change churches, or make new friends. I wanted to be free from those unhealthy relationship patterns that were robbing me physically, mentally, and emotionally.

This was a huge decision for me, since I had always cared about what everyone thought and had avoided conflict at all costs. I had also thought that was what it meant to be a good Christian—to comply, to keep the peace at all costs.

But when you are diagnosed with a life-threatening disease, everything you believe gets jolted. You go into survival mode just to live. Sometimes it takes a crisis (or huge interruption) to change your mindset.

My new mantra was the word "no." I swung from one extreme to another. I went from always "yes" to "stick it." I no longer cared if everyone around me was angry. I was terrified I was going to lose my colon, and that took precedence over any unhealthy relationship. I only had enough energy to take care of my kids (barely) and myself.

Unfortunately, those around me were not used to the new protocol. I told my parents off a few times. In just a few conversations, I unleashed 40 years of anger. As you can imagine, that didn't go over well. They didn't understand there was an enormous amount of hidden anger that had been suppressed all this time. I had suddenly changed the dynamics of our relationship, and they didn't like it. I, on the other hand, finally felt free. I couldn't wait to tell them off again. Sadly, I was like a volcano erupting and spewing hot lava on anyone in my vicinity. The little child inside of me had newfound power; it was exhilarating.

Maybe you can relate to my story. It may be different from mine, but there could be common themes. You might feel invisible. Maybe you have been trying to please everyone, and in the process, you have lost yourself. Maybe you are irritated or even angry because your spouse doesn't understand you. Perhaps you continually lose your temper with everyone in your path. Or you stuff your feelings. Maybe you even blame God for your situation. He could have stepped in, but He didn't. He's silent, and you feel abandoned. Perhaps you are stuck in a cycle of lies about yourself. Whatever the situation, you are living in one big "interruption."

Let me assure you that God is right there in the midst of your situation. While you may not feel or see Him right now, He is working to bring you to a better place. It may be that you need to address hurts that are raw and heal open wounds.

Neither Andy nor I realized how devastating the wounds from the past would be. I never expected my buried pain to exact such a costly toll. But the hard things came, and our marriage was severely interrupted.

REFLECTION

1. Are you wondering where God is in your situation?
2. Are you so angry or disillusioned that you have left your faith? Or perhaps you are cynical and assume God loves everyone, just not you?
3. In what ways do you feel your spouse doesn't understand you?
4. In what areas are you having a hard time setting boundaries with your spouse? With your family?
5. List some healthy boundaries you can set with others starting today.

CHAPTER REVIEW

1. Setting healthy boundaries is imperative so you don't say "yes" to things God didn't call you to do.
2. It is better to be honest about your feelings than continue to hide them and skirt around difficult issues.
3. Buried pain will take a toll on your marriage one way or another.
4. God loves you and has not left you. Don't leave Him.

VERSE FOR SPIRITUAL WARFARE

James 1:12

"Blessed is the one who perseveres under trial because, having stood the test, that person will receive the crown of life that the LORD has promised to those who love him."

PRAYER

God, I don't always understand Your ways, but I know I can trust You with my deepest pain. Whenever I doubt, help my unbelief. Even though my life hasn't turned out exactly as I expected, You are not surprised. Give me the grace to walk through these interruptions knowing You are a good God. That You will work all things out for Your glory, in Christ Jesus. I ask You to give me a positive outlook, a fresh perspective where my judgment has been clouded. Give me supernatural eyes to see the things You see. Where I have lost hope, restore the joy of my salvation. I recommit my life to You. Help me grow more passionate about You every day through prayer and worship. Give me the discipline to read Your word, even when I feel discouraged. Most of all, give me the strength to apply Your words to my life so there is a behavior change.

CHAPTER 6

Marriage Interrupted

"What appears to be an interruption is often an intervention."
—Rich Wilkerson, Jr.

After the Crohn's diagnosis, I was desperately seeking all remedies for my sick colon. I knew I only had a short time to turn things around before I would need a colostomy, an irreversible procedure that would remove my colon. The doctor recommended that I remove all stress from my life, as this would give me the best chance to heal.

After several heated conversations with my parents and a few futile counseling sessions with a family counselor, Andy and I agreed there was nothing left to do but leave my family. Truthfully, I think we all needed some peace.

Together, Andy and I told my parents never to contact us or our kids again. Ever. No presents, cards, calls, or visits. Nothing. Here I was repeating the very thing I swore I would never repeat—family estrangement.

After we broke off the relationship with my parents, reality set in. Andy and I worried we would be judged harshly by other family and friends, especially those who professed to be Christians. I was angry I had been painted into such an impossible corner. Neither of us wanted to choose estrangement; sadly, it seemed to have chosen us. My family of origin had completely broken down with no hope of recovery. We had exhausted every avenue with my parents. How could this happen to a Christian family, especially one who had been in ministry for over 30 years?

I also worried I was causing others to think things of my parents that were untrue. I was not actually the first child to leave the family. My older sister had left several years earlier. Many people assumed some kind of sexual dysfunction had led to both my sister's and my estrangement. This was not the case. I felt guilty that I was contributing to this shadow that would be cast on my parents.

I entered this estrangement with a lot of faulty assumptions. Truthfully, I thought it would last for six months. Possibly a year. Perhaps my leaving would jolt them into change, especially since I was the second child to leave. In the back of my head, I thought God would miraculously reveal to them the real problem. Or that God would heal me, and everyone would say they were sorry. And then we would live happily ever after. Most of all, I thought Andy would magically jump inside my head and understand all my feelings. None of this happened, which only made me angrier at him and God.

The truth was we did not have the tools to deal with all the dysfunctions in my family of origin. I was constantly stirred up by new situations, replaying them over and over in my head, each scene in 3D, like a bad rerun. In turn, it triggered a new level of sickness; I was falling into an abyss, never to return.

Nevertheless, Andy and I questioned our decision to leave the family for many years after the break. Over and over, we kept trying to figure out what happened, or how we could have done things differently. It was a cycle of difficult questions that came back to the same frustrating answer. There was no answer.

Looking back, I now realize my family of origin broke down because we did not know how to deal with conflict in a healthy way. I think we all thought that being a Christian was enough—no other work was required. In reality, we lacked skills in setting boundaries, harbored unforgiveness, had unrealistic expectations, blamed others when we needed to take ownership, and extended very little grace. Anger ruled. Pride kept everyone from coming together. Self-protection was more important than family unity.

Unfortunately, those generational sins had been passed down to me and were interfering in our marriage. Thankfully, Andy agreed to go with me to see a marriage counselor. We had a lot to work through—both external and internal stressors that we needed to address. I think he finally realized dodging pre-marital counseling was not the best idea. "Pushing through" wasn't going to cut it this time.

Our marriage had been interrupted by a demanding job with a boss who had no boundaries, an illness that seemed irreversible, and an estrangement from my extended family. Ultimately, though, it had been interrupted by our own poor communication and unhealthy coping mechanisms. None of it was convenient or welcomed. But it came anyway.

It seemed like one minute we were just two kids in high school, madly in love with each other, and the next minute we were swirling in a vortex that was sucking us down into a dark hole.

Secretly, I couldn't wait to sit down with the counselor and watch him go after Andy. I was convinced I was in the right. After all, I was the one suffering from a health crisis and past family trauma. Surely the counselor would tell Andy to back off—perhaps even give him a guilt trip for working too much and quote a few Bible verses for good measure.

I, on the other hand, would sit quietly and try to act humbly while basking in my glorious vindication. My deliverance was coming. It was so close I could taste it. Boy, did I have a rude awakening.

Our first session seemed to go well. Chuck, our counselor, did confront Andy about a few things, which made me feel validated. But after about four sessions, Chuck told me he wanted me to come back alone without Andy.

I was furious. Andy was the problem. I couldn't understand why he needed to see me without Andy. He was supposed to be concentrating on Andy, not me! At the time, I didn't realize it was standard protocol to talk with each spouse alone after you meet for a few sessions. I think I may have overreacted.

Begrudgingly, I went alone. I think Andy was probably elated he was off the hook for the time being. I'm sure it probably validated his underlying thoughts that I was the problem. I decided I no longer liked Chuck, but I was a little intrigued because I knew I hadn't done anything wrong. I was the people-pleaser, for heaven's sake. (Like that was a good thing.)

In my mind, I envisioned us talking about how we were going to change Andy. I am embarrassed to say that I had it all planned out. Chuck, with his long list of notes, would tell me what a wonderful wife I had been. Obviously, we would need to work together to come up with a great strategy to fix Andy.

Yeah, that didn't happen.

Some conversations in your life are so shocking you will never forget them. This was one of those conversations. I was hit with a sledgehammer. What Chuck had to say had nothing at all to do with Andy. It had everything to do with me.

He told me I needed to start expressing my feelings, setting boundaries, and dealing honestly with myself and everyone around me—even if it made them uncomfortable or angry. Furthermore, he pointed out I was internalizing everything to the point of no return. If I didn't change, I would be dead in a year. That part was shocking. I don't know if Chuck was being overdramatic. He wasn't a medical doctor. But he had seen enough people in his practice to know the way I was dealing with my problems was not only toxic but life-threatening.

After all that, he said I needed to work through my childhood issues. There were serious generational strongholds in my family that were causing me great harm. Although I agreed on some level with Chuck's assessment, I was angry that I had to do the work. It wasn't my fault. I was clearly the victim. Why should I be the one to change my behavior? Everyone else needed to change, not me. I also worried if I changed my behavior too much it would cause additional conflict with Andy. At that time in my life, I couldn't handle Andy being angry with me. Especially since we had already broken things off with my family.

I politely listened to Chuck for the hour, and then I walked out the door. I hated Chuck. He ruined all my plans.

Andy went to see him a few more times after that, and then we quit going to counseling. I decided Chuck didn't know what he was talking about. I convinced myself he was a bad counselor. Sadly, I was still caught in the mindset that everyone else was to blame. I had no power of my own, no one understood or loved me, and I was worthless. I wasn't in a place to hear the truth.

So, we treaded water for another six months. We were stuck. And, as you can guess, the problems did not magically disappear. Neither did God deliver me from my illness, even though I had prayed fervently.

I did not like or understand God; it seemed He was up in heaven pulling levers like a crazy scientist or madman who had just been given permission to destroy my life.

I also wondered if my suffering was payback for something I had done. I could not see God as a good, loving Father who suffered and hurt with me. Instead, I saw Him as the instigator of all my pain. I saw Him as cruel, mean, and unloving. I felt like a pawn in a sick game of chess. I equated God's silence with abandonment.

After a while, the guilt, anger, and confusion were more abundant than ever. In addition to our marital discord, Andy and I had never imagined how difficult it would be to walk away from my family. It was awkward at holidays. We struggled to explain it to friends.

Our kids were confused. They had lost cousins and one set of grandparents overnight. I swore I would not do this to my kids. I knew firsthand what it was like to lose family members and about the abandonment issues that followed. Yet here I was doing the same thing. History had repeated itself. We traded one set of problems for another; it felt so shameful. And I suffered with an enormous amount of guilt.

Truthfully, God allowed the three simultaneous and major problems—job issues, health issues, and a family estrangement—to help us break free from unhealthy thought patterns and behaviors. God interrupted our marriage to save us.

If you are struggling in your marriage, keep reading! Part II of this book focuses on the big picture. We will look at the garden of Eden and discuss God's design for marriage. More importantly, I offer practical suggestions to help you address conflict in your marriage. With the help of these proven tools and through the power of the Holy Spirit, I am confident you will see real, lasting change.

REFLECTION

1. What, if anything, has interrupted your marriage?
2. Have you and your spouse truly cleaved to one another?
3. In what ways are you angry at God for your season of suffering?
4. How will you deal with your issues? Do you need extra help?
5. Is pride hindering you from admitting your part in the equation?

CHAPTER REVIEW

1. God does not force us to change our behavior.
2. Pride keeps us from focusing on our own problems and causes us to blame others instead.
3. Internalizing anger is not sustainable.
4. Leaving and cleaving is not only biblical but also imperative if you want a strong marriage.

VERSES FOR SPIRITUAL WARFARE

Genesis 2:24

"This is why a man leaves his father and mother and is united to his wife, and they become one flesh."

Romans 12:10

"Be devoted to one another in love. Honor one another above yourselves."

PRAYER

God, I pray You would give me and my spouse the ears to hear and the eyes to see our own faults. I pray we would stop blaming each other. Help us to focus on what we have the power to change—ourselves. Teach us how to love each other well. Show us how to leave father and mother and truly cling to each other so we will not be divided. I ask that we leave pride at the door as we are convicted of wrongful behaviors. Let us both release any hidden anger that may be keeping us from sitting down and talking to each other in an appropriate manner. Thank You for helping us to be devoted to each other in love by putting the other person first, despite what we may feel at the time. If we need help navigating our issues, provide a godly counselor who can help us reveal blind spots we may have. I pray we will not quit when it gets hard, even though it may be painful. Thank You for blessing our marriage.

PART II

REDEEMED

CHAPTER 7

Through the Doors of Eden

"We all long for Eden, and we are constantly glimpsing it: our whole nature at its best and least corrupted, its gentlest and most human, is still soaked with the sense of exile."

—J.R.R. Tolkien,
The Letters of J.R.R. Tolkien

It was six weeks before our wedding day. My lease was up at my apartment, so Andy let me move into his condo while he graciously moved back home with his parents. It was a perfect plan. I would spend the remaining time before the "big day" sprucing up our home so it would be ready to live in as a couple.

I spent hours with a decorator friend who helped me pick out just the right paint colors, stain for the wood floors, window treatments, etc. I registered for wedding gifts at all the right places to get matching bedding, plates, and miscellaneous home décor for all 600 square feet.

One of the things the decorator recommended was to remove two doors in the hall area to add more space. Andy gladly took the doors off the hinges for me, but for some reason he wouldn't haul them off to the dumpster outside our condo. After I asked him several times, he finally admitted he wanted to make the doors into coffee tables; however, I could not visualize two doors turned sideways looking any better than they did upright. They were ugly in either direction. More importantly, they were an impediment to my grand plan.

After several weeks of staring at the two impertinent doors leaning against the living room wall in my tiny condo, I finally got irritated and decided to move (dump) them myself without telling Andy. So, one Saturday, I grabbed a door and proceeded to haul it to the dumpster.

Nope. No coffee table doors in my living room. Andy isn't telling me what to do!

Unfortunately, my lack of agility caught up with me once again. As I was walking out, I tripped down the three steps in front of our building. The heavy door pulled me down the stairs, and my ankle twisted in all sorts of directions. It was so painful that when I landed on the ground, I momentarily blacked out. When I came to, I was immediately nauseated and threw up right next to the steps. (Oddly, this was just outside where the muffin incident would happen three months later. It was an omen.)

One of Andy's friends happened to drive up just as I was getting sick. He quickly got out of the car, moved the door out of the way, and took me straight to the emergency room, leaving the remnants of "yesterday's lunch" for everyone to sidestep.

When I arrived at the hospital, I was in horrific pain. Eventually the doctor saw me and said I had torn ligaments in my ankle. They fitted me with a large boot and sent me home with crutches.

I was horrified. No bride wants to make her wedding debut in crutches and a boot the size of Godzilla's foot.

I was also angry at Andy, but since we were getting married in six weeks, I stuffed it down. We never spoke of the door situation again. He knew when he was beat. That afternoon, Andy disposed of the doors. But my ankle injury was a big price to pay for me getting my way.

Thankfully, our wedding day was not ruined. My ankle healed just enough that, with the help of my father and an ankle brace, I made it down the aisle just fine.

Looking back, I realize we spent a lot of time and money physically preparing the environment of our home. The focus was external rather than internal. We didn't know what else to do. It never occurred to us that we needed to talk about what really happened in the door situation. Both Andy and I could have handled it better. He let the doors sit in our living room for a long time. I tried to sneak off and dump them without telling him. Andy was passive. I was aggressive. The practice of deferring to each other was not yet a reality in our relationship. This would take years to refine because, let's face it, dying to self doesn't come naturally.

When you walk down the aisle, you think you are finally going to get all of your needs met, but it is not quite that way. Marriage is about meeting the needs of your spouse first. It is the way of the cross.

God gave us a blueprint to help us understand these difficult concepts when He created Adam and Eve. Let's look more closely in Genesis to see the perfect environment before sin entered the world.

GOD'S ORIGINAL BLUEPRINT FOR MARRIAGE—EDEN

The first two chapters of Genesis are the only chapters in the entire Bible where the union of God and man and the union of woman and man are uncorrupted by sin. This seems like an important concept to me. It reveal's God's blueprint for marriage. Dr. David Jeremiah says in his study notes that the union of man and woman is the "only human institution that God created before the Fall" (page 7).

Once you study the concepts from the Genesis account of the garden of Eden and understand God's lavish love for His children, it is much harder to cherry-pick verses from Ephesians 5 and Colossians 3 (the household codes) and twist them for the purpose of control or dominance. We are all called to die to self just as Jesus did (Gal. 5:24).

From the world's standpoint, dying to self looks ridiculous. But the world doesn't understand that in order to find life, you must first give it up. Matthew 16:24–25 says:

> Then Jesus said to his disciples, "Whoever wants to be my disciple must deny themselves and take up their cross

and follow me. For whoever wants to save their life will lose it, but whoever loses their life for me will find it."

So, let's look closely at the garden of Eden. I think you will see the same things I see. The perfect environment God created for Adam and Eve reveals both God's character and His intentions for marriage. It helps us see how man and woman worked together with God, not everyone against each other. Furthermore, Jesus (our greatest example) is the personification of that love in the New Testament. Marriage reflects the heart of the gospel. The scarlet thread of Christ's sacrificial love can be traced throughout all of human history—from the beginning of time in the garden until today, as we await His return. Hang on here! This analysis of creation will tie into marriage more than you realize.

Light

The first thing God did on day one of creation was speak light into existence. And then He separated the light from the darkness. On the fourth day of creation, He created the sun, moon, and stars to provide light for both day and night.

In a similar way, Jesus Christ, "the light of all mankind" (John 1:4), needs to come first within a marriage relationship. Without the light of Christ, you cannot be the spouse you were truly called to be. Light brings revelation. It allows us to know and be known authentically. Marriage is about reflecting Jesus, not being the light ourselves. Self-centered and proud people make poor spouses.

Have you and your spouse both accepted Jesus Christ, the eternal light, as Lord of your lives? Are you actively growing in your faith? Do you attend church together? Do you act like Christians publicly and privately?

Boundaries

God is a God of order, not chaos. In fact, the creation story tells us He brought order out of the formless in Genesis 1. If you look at some of the repeated statements in the creation narrative, you will notice how God separated one thing from the other: light from darkness, heavens from earth, land from sea, day from night. He set boundaries and said those boundaries were "good."

Why did God put boundaries in place? I believe it was to protect the first couple, Adam and Eve (and eventually to protect us). God put them in a safe and orderly world so they would thrive, not merely survive.

Without boundaries, there would be chaos, even to the point of death. Water would overtake the land, darkness would overtake the light, the atmosphere would mingle with space, and there would be no separation between the heavens and earth. God lovingly created a beautiful and safe environment in the beginning for Adam and Eve using boundaries for their protection.

In the New Testament, Jesus set boundaries many times. He walked away from crowds, He separated Himself to be alone with God, He said "no," and in one story He didn't give in to His mother and brothers. These are only a few examples.

Jesus pleased God, not man. (We will talk more about people-pleasing in the next chapter.)

It is biblical to have boundaries.

Does your home environment reflect the same kind of love that God displayed for us in creation? Do you respect each other equally? Are there healthy boundaries—physically, emotionally, mentally, and spiritually—in place? Is it chaotic? Does everyone feel safe? Do your children see you prioritize your marriage relationship as second only to God?

Provision

God is our provider. In creation, He gave His children good gifts not only for sustenance, but also for pleasure. He made sure Adam and Eve were taken care of physically when He breathed life into their nostrils.

He could have created Adam and Eve on day one, but that world would not have sustained life. He waited until day six so they would have all they needed to live. God lovingly provided for His beloved creation like a good father provides for his children.

Do you take care of those you love like God took care of Adam and Eve? Do you sacrificially make provisions for your family? Do you plan for the future? Do you save, tithe, and spend within your means? First Timothy 5:8 says:

> Anyone who does not provide for their relatives, and especially for their own household, has denied the faith and is worse than an unbeliever.

Life

God is the giver of life. If you look at creation, you see joy, energy, color, beauty, and fruitfulness brimming everywhere. God spoke life into being just with His words. Can you imagine creating life just by speaking? You may not realize it, but your words are also powerful. Death and life are in the power of the tongue (Prov. 18:21).

In the New Testament, Jesus died for us so we might have life. This is the kind of sacrificial love God wants us to have for each other.

Is your household joyful and positive? Are you creating life with your words, or are they destructive, even critical? Do you protect each other emotionally? Do you use your words to punish, blame, seek revenge, or deceive? Are you encouraging or discouraging your spouse? Do you respect your spouse or treat him or her with indifference, even contempt?

Goodness

God is good. And He says His creation was good seven times throughout the creation account (Gen. 1:4, 10, 12, 18, 21, 25, 31). Even creation itself cries out that God is good.

When Adam and Eve were placed in the garden of Eden, they were surrounded by His goodness. But they also had free wills and could choose whether or not to replicate His goodness in their own lives.

God never tainted His creation with manipulation, threats, or demands in exchange for His goodness; it was a gift freely given. If God were to exhibit this type of behavior, He would no longer be good. In fact, He would be controlling and abusive like Satan.

In a marriage relationship, the husband is to be so kind and good to his wife that she naturally chooses to listen to him.

Let me make this clear: biblical submission in marriage begins with the husband's willingness to lay down his life for his wife. This includes protecting her if she is in physical danger, but also sacrificially dying to his flesh daily. It means being kind in words and deeds.

If a wife is struggling with following her husband, it could be the husband does not understand how to cherish his wife. Who would want to follow someone who is mean, selfish, controlling, or even cruel? It makes no sense.

God is very clear about how husbands are to treat their wives. He even tells husbands their prayers will not be answered if they are not considerate and respectful to their wives. First Peter 3:7 says:

> Husbands, in the same way be considerate as you live with your wives and treat them with respect as the weaker partner and as heirs with you of the gracious gift of life, so that nothing will hinder your prayers.

Biblical submission is easiest when both husband and wife are good to each other, die to self regularly, work as a team, and lovingly respect each other. First Corinthians 10:24 says: "No one should seek their own good, but the good of others."

Are you kind and good to your spouse? Do you die to yourself daily? Do you put your spouse's needs first? Are you working together as a team? Do you respect each other?

Love

God is love. He lovingly created Adam and Eve to commune with Him daily. They had a relationship with Him in the garden of Eden unlike anything we have ever experienced. All they ever knew was God's lavish, holy love.

It must have been glorious during this time. A world made for two people united in a perfect love. In deep and symbolic ways, the love of God revealed through the marriage union of Adam and Eve illustrated the love of Christ Jesus for His bride, the Church (Eph. 5:25).

Ever since, our hearts have been yearning to recover this paradise lost. We long to be completely loved, naked, vulnerable, and unashamed before each other and God.

Is God's love the focal point of your marriage? Are you vulnerable with each other? Are you naked and unashamed? Are you making love regularly? Do you use sex as a weapon? Does your love, as well as God's love, permeate your home unconditionally?

HEALTHY MARRIAGES REFLECT GOD'S GOOD CREATED ORDER

Although we can never recover all that has been lost in the garden (until Christ returns!), I do believe we can have healthy marriages that reflect God's good, created order now. It is a balance and rhythm that can be achieved over time if both husband and wife are regularly in fellowship with God and submitting to His will.

In order for a biblical marriage to fully work, the husband needs to be in submission to God first. Then he can successfully take the lead spiritually as head of the home. God goes a step further and tells the wife to put her husband first even if he is not a believer. Perhaps her conduct will lead him to the Lord (1 Pet. 3:1–2). This is not easy! Consistently, we see how the Bible redirects us to always do the right thing even if the other person does not choose to behave according to Scripture.

In turn, the husband is responsible for how he leads. Adam was clearly told to be the leader in the garden. Genesis 2:15 says: "Then the LORD God placed the man in the garden of Eden to cultivate it and guard it" (GNT). In fact, Adam's first assignment was to name the animals and be in charge of them before Eve ever existed.

From this verse, we directly see the role of headship was a product of God's good, created order given to Adam before the fall of mankind. This was about order, not value. Furthermore, God Himself showed Adam how to lead when they walked together in the garden daily; it was a relationship of lavish love with boundaries (don't eat the fruit).

Another clue to headship is that when sin entered the garden, God specifically called out Adam first, not Eve. Genesis 3:9 says: "The LORD God called to the man, 'Where are you?'"

Adam spends the next few verses trying to rationalize his sin by blaming both God and Eve in one fell swoop. Genesis 3:12 says, "The man said, 'the woman you put here with me—she gave me some fruit from the tree, and I ate it.'" There would have been no need to blame Eve if he did not feel responsible for the garden in the first place. He knew he was culpable. Ultimately, Adam blamed God. It was His fault He made Eve in the first place. (I'd love to point fingers here but I, too, have blamed God for my problems.)

I would also like to point out that when Adam was given headship of the garden, there were no generational curses or bents passed down to him from human parents. God was his parent and mentor! Blaming God, our spouses, or even our parents for our own failures will never remedy the situation. We must take full responsibility for our shortcomings to get healing.

After God confronted both Adam and Eve, they received curses for crossing the boundaries (sin) God set in place. Specifically, one of Eve's curses was that she would desire to control her husband. On the other hand, the husband would be tempted to lead poorly, even harshly. There would be a temptation for role reversal of husband and wife. Genesis 3:16 (NLT) says:

> Then he said to the woman, "I will sharpen the pain of your pregnancy, and in pain you will give birth. And you will desire to control your husband, but he will rule over you."

The desire to control her husband and being treated harshly (rule) in headship were the curses. Not headship itself, which was already in place before the fall. One of the main struggles of married couples is leading and following without the sin of control or passivity. The "door story" at the beginning of this chapter is just one example of how easily we default to role reversal because of our sin nature.

The good news is that Christ's death changed the curse of sin. We don't have to give in to control or passivity because we now have the Holy Spirit to help us have a healthy marriage where both husband and wife do not blame each other, rather they take responsibility for their own actions and ask for forgiveness when wrong. Thankfully, this beautiful model still leaves room for disagreements and boundaries.

HEALTHY MARRIAGES GIVE EQUAL VALUE TO THEIR ROLES

The role of the husband and wife are a dicey subject in today's culture; however, it shouldn't be that controversial because God constantly uplifts both men and women in the Bible. Let's pick up in Genesis 2:20 after Adam names the animals. It is then Adam realizes he doesn't have a pair or a complement like everyone else on the planet. It says: The man gave names to all the livestock, to the birds of the sky, and to every wild animal; but for the man no helper was found as his complement. (HCSB)

God said it wasn't good for Adam to be alone, so He built a woman. He fashioned her by hand using the rib from Adam's side (Gen. 2:18–21).

There are two important concepts we need to understand from these verses.

The first concept is God said it wasn't good for man to be alone, so He took a rib from the side of Adam to create Eve. She wasn't made separately like all the other creatures; she was taken from Adam. When God made her, He did not take a bone from Adam's foot, toe, hand, finger, or his head; it was from his side. Eve was made to go alongside Adam as a beautiful reminder that she was part of his flesh. Who treats their flesh badly?

The second concept is God breathed life into every other creature, but He fashioned or built the woman by hand. He took His time because she was worth the extra effort. She was neither more powerful nor worthless when He made her; she was a complement and a helper with great power of her own.

One of the worst fallacies is that women are either doormats or liberated from any type of accountability to their husbands. *The Jeremiah Study Bible* study notes says this about women:

> The woman was his helper (or 'help meet,' with the sense of corresponding precisely to him)—one who supplied strengths that Adam lacked. The Hebrew term does not imply that the helper is weaker or less valuable than the one who is helped. In fact, in Hebrew, help is a word

of power. The woman is a 'power' matching the man! (page 8).

Did you know the Holy Spirit, who is an integral part of the Trinity, is also referred to as the "Helper" (John 14:26). He is the one who gives power and strength to us. The Amplified Bible calls the Helper (Holy Spirit) a "comforter, advocate, intercessor, counselor, strengthener, standby."

The Bible never refers to the Holy Spirit as any less important than Jesus or God because the Trinity is about order, not about who is more valuable. They all work together as a team in perfect union, each providing different roles (Matt. 28:19).

While the wife is certainly not the Holy Spirit, her role as the "helper" is not any less valuable than the husband's role. She brings strength, comfort, intercessory prayer and many other wonderful things to the union! Marriage, like the Trinity, is a relationship with different roles: God, husband, and wife all working together in perfect union.

Can you imagine what it would be like if God the Father, God the Son, and God the Holy Spirit were fighting with each other about their roles? It would be disastrous! It would be a cosmic war, utterly out of balance, destroying not only each other but everything in their path, including us.

Obviously, this would never happen because the Trinity is always in perfect union and balance, but it does make you think about what happens when our marriages get out of sync with God. That is disastrous. We destroy each other and everything in our path because we are no longer working together, as a couple, like God originally designed. Marriage is a team sport. Ephesians 5:21 says, "Submit to one another out of reverence to Christ."

There is a balance between God, husband, and wife that reflects the Trinity. In the garden, it was a perfect union that deferred to each other in complete love without sin. We can still strive for this same balance in our marriage relationships (with God's help) if we will defer to each other with the same love and goodness God modeled first.

WILL YOU FOLLOW GOD'S BLUEPRINT?

The one thing I want to emphasize in this book is how much God loves His bride, the Church (us). The groom (Jesus) was willing to die for His bride—not control, demean, abuse, or hurt her in any way. This is our example for marriage.

Before you draw your own conclusions, I encourage you to pray about your roles as husband and wife. Search the Bible. Many times, we want God's guidance and yet we resent it at the same time because it goes against our will, our flesh.

God knew what He was doing when He showcased His glory both in the original creation and later through the incarnation of Jesus Christ, the Son of God. Genesis 1–2 is not just a good story; it is the original blueprint for marriage and should be your guide for a healthy relationship. Until Christ's return, we long for the perfection of Eden.

Dr. David Jeremiah says this:

The entire world groans for Eden to be re-created. When Christ returns to rule and reign on this earth during the Millennium, life will resume as it was before the curse (Ps. 65). The full resolution will be in the eternal state (Rev. 21-22). (page 10)

One day Jesus will restore His creation when He comes back for us, His bride. This truly is the greatest love story of all time. This can be your love story too.

REFLECTION

1. In what ways do you feel you have a healthy marriage, in accordance with God's design?

2. In what ways does your marriage *not* reflect God's perfect design?

3. List ways you can change the environment of your home to reflect the template God set in creation.

4. How do you feel about the roles of husband and wife?

5. If you don't want to follow God's template, why?

CHAPTER REVIEW

1. God gave couples a blueprint for marriage in creation.

2. Submitting to each other in love can and should coexist in a marriage.

3. God's created order and Christ's relationship with His bride (us) to help us better understand Christian marriage.

VERSES FOR SPIRITUAL WARFARE

1 Peter 4:8

"Above all, love each other deeply, because love covers over a multitude of sins."

John 15:13

"Greater love has no one than this: to lay down one's life for one's friends."

PRAYER

God, thank You for designing a perfect world before sin so that we could look to it for inspiration, confirmation, and direction when it comes to our own marriages. Help us to see that unconditional love is at the center of all You do from the beginning of time until now. Show us how to replicate this kind of love with each other.

Help us as a couple to submit to Your will first, and then to submit to each other in love. I pray there will be no temptation to take scriptures out of context to justify threats, bullying, or dominance. Instead, let us defer to each other in love, considering the needs of the other before ourselves. Thank You, God, for giving us wisdom to navigate this difficult area so we are one.

CHAPTER 8

People-Pleasing Pizza

"One of the greatest gifts you can give your husband is your own wholeness."

—Stormie Omartian,
The Power of a Praying Wife

Before I married Andy, there was another guy. Although he was a nice guy, he wasn't the one for me. Thinking back, I am sure it went downhill after the "pizza incident." Like a good Italian, I decided to show off my cooking skills and make a homemade pizza for dinner. I spent hours slaving in the kitchen, trying to prove my worth as a person and potential wife.

I started early in the morning prepping, cutting, and cooking so the homemade pizza would be ready by that evening. I sweated, worried, and dreamed of a perfect evening with this man who would think I was the best cook ever, even better than his mother.

If you know anything about homemade pizza, you know it is a big deal to work with yeast. There is the kneading, the rising, and the rolling out of the dough to make the crust just right. Then there's the sauce. There's lots of cooking and simmering to get the perfect consistency. And the flavor must be savory, with a tiny bit of sweetness—the perfect balance.

Sadly, I was obsessed with perfection. My self-image was wrapped up in this wad of dough laced with tomatoes. Sounds silly now. When this young man came over that evening, I had the pizza ready for us to eat; it was beautiful.

We sat down at the dinner table, prayed, and then started eating. I thought the pizza was heavenly. On the other hand, this young man casually stated that it was about as good as Pizza Hut. Pizza Hut? Are you kidding me? I wanted to slap him upside the head with the pizza dough … or dunk him in a vat of olive oil. Okay, not really. But I at least wanted him to acknowledge how much I slaved in the kitchen for him and be grateful for what I did.

I was devastated that night. I valued his opinion so much that it made me question my worth and my ability to cook. So much that I never made homemade pizza again.

Not long after "pizza-gate," I had the good sense to break up with him. I realized it would be difficult to be in a relationship with someone who didn't value me or my efforts.

I guess the pizza served its purpose; it showed me he was low on love and gratitude. Not a good recipe for a healthy marriage. Thankfully, I married someone who is very grateful for my ability to cook and who values me and my time!

This pizza story is just one small incident in my lifetime of people-pleasing. When I got married, I expected my husband to give me constant approval and validation. He was supposed to tell me who I was as a person; however, he thought I already knew. He didn't get the "propping-up" memo. So, my worth ebbed and flowed depending upon whatever happened that day. It hinged on whatever anyone said to me—Andy most of all.

When Andy didn't validate or approve of me, I often swung in the other direction. I was angry, pouted, and became defensive. I was one big emotional roller coaster that was rooted in the latest feelings instead of God's truth. To be honest, I was surprised and confused when I reacted in such childish ways because I truly did not want to behave in that manner.

Perhaps you do the same thing. You don't get the validation you want through people-pleasing, so you react strongly, maybe even with revenge. Perhaps you try to manipulate your spouse into loving you or issue threats in order to get your needs met. You may even be somewhat emotionally aggressive without realizing it. Perhaps even a bully.

Others of you may be more of a loner. You don't create drama, but you also don't open up. You would rather contain your feelings in your brain to maintain control of your world. You would rather handle it all than bother those around you with your problems.

Practicing emotional intimacy doesn't come naturally because, most likely, you weren't encouraged to do it while growing up. So, you live on an "island" while your spouse is begging for you to share yourself in more emotionally intimate ways.

Whether you are a people-pleaser, emotionally aggressive, a loner, or all three, your spouse is not a mind reader. You have to be naked emotionally to know and be known. The danger of not being emotionally transparent is that your spouse doesn't know who you are as a person. Therefore, you won't reap the benefits of what true marriage looks and feels like—being "one" as a couple.

So how do you get out of this cycle? How do you show up in your marriage as a healthy adult, knowing that no matter what your spouse says, you are valuable as a person?

PEOPLE-PLEASING AND WORTH

I've learned over the years that too many people determine their worth based on what others say or who they have pleased. While a good reputation is important (and biblical) it cannot be the foundation of your belief system. Your worth needs to be rooted in truth so that when you say something your spouse doesn't agree with, it is okay. Additionally, you don't have to run away, retaliate, or emotionally withdraw when you feel hurt.

You can think about worth in two different ways: man's idea of worth versus God's idea of worth.

The Cambridge Dictionary defines worth as "the importance or usefulness of someone or something." Many times, worth also implies a dollar value. This is a horrible way to define it when talking about people. I don't want to be valued simply by my usefulness or how much I have in the bank.

God's definition is so much better; it is based on nothing we do. We are worthy of love just because God chose to love

People-Pleasing Pizza

us. We can't earn that status, which means we also can't lose it. Thank the Lord!

> For it is by grace you have been saved, through faith—
> and this is not from yourselves, it is the gift of God—not
> by works, so that no one can boast. (Ephesians 2:8–9)

If you are struggling with the idea of your own worth, you may be focusing on man's definition instead of God's definition. Here is a quiz to help you decide if you are looking to others to define your worth:

1. Are you often angry or resentful about being pushed into something you didn't want to do?
2. Do you stay quiet because you think your ideas and opinions are stupid or embarrassing?
3. Do you go to extremes to keep peace at all costs?
4. Are you prone to saying "yes" without thinking first?
5. Do you neglect your needs over the needs of others?
6. Are you angry at yourself when you don't speak up?
7. Do you feel embarrassed after you do speak up, wishing you never said anything?
8. Do you feel that your personal ambitions are silly or embarrassing?
9. Do you feel guilty for saying "no"?

10. Do you give up easily when you are not perfect?

11. Do you take the blame for things you didn't do?

If you said "yes" to most of the questions, then you might be struggling with people-pleasing. In other words, you value self-protection more than believing the truth about your worth as a believer in Christ.

PEOPLE-PLEASING IN YOUR MARRIAGE

Satan's top three lies that he loves to tell are that we are unloved, powerless, and worthless. You can see from our discussion of worth how this struggle might play out in a marriage. Maybe you are always looking for your spouse's approval. When you don't get it, you immediately feel shame. You think you are not enough or that you are worthless. Maybe you feel unloved, so you try harder to get your needs met.

Even the best marriages have times of conflict. It's okay. The most important thing to realize is that your spouse was never designed to provide you with worth. No person can do that. Nor were you designed to manage everyone's emotions in order to achieve your desired outcome.

In their book *Vertical Marriage*, Dave and Ann Wilson say this:

> But again, if you think that they [your spouse] are finally going to completely give you what you need, you'll be hurt, frustrated, and bitter ... because they were never

made to fill you. Even at their best, your expectations need to be appropriately tempered. Because only God can fill you. (page 84)

Your worth is from God, not man. As a recovering people-pleaser, it is still hard for me. I'm tempted to feel ashamed when I don't get a desired outcome. I want my husband to be happy with me at all times. I deeply want to be loved for my works and feel "enough" because of what I do. It's only natural. But sooner or later I will fail him.

As marriage partners, we certainly need to cheer each other on, but when that doesn't happen, we can know God still sees us and loves us. He is our ultimate love and firm foundation. We are His, despite any opinion of others, even our own spouses.

Dr. David Jeremiah (*The Jeremiah Study Bible*) says this in his study notes about shame and people-pleasing:

> Minus sin, the first married couple was not ashamed. There was no self-consciousness or anxiety about what the other person thought; husband and wife were perfectly secure with one another. God designed marriage for this. (page 9)

If you have been wrapped up in man's definition of worth, take a deep breath. There is a better way.

HOW TO BE VULNERABLE WITH YOUR SPOUSE

If you want to truly connect with your spouse, you might need to adjust a few things in your life. Like me, you may know all the right answers, but you just can't get there. You are stuck. Here are some tips.

Stop Burying Your Feelings
Burying your feelings can lead to horrible side effects that manifest mentally, physically, spiritually, and emotionally. God gave us feelings; it is important to express them appropriately and work through them together as a couple. When this doesn't happen, resentment, bitterness, and anger seep out.

If you have been burying your feelings for a long time, you may be tempted to explode. Don't be like the woman who "randomly" walked away from her marriage after 25 years because she had one big explosion. The husband is left shocked because he never knew there was a problem.

It is important to temper your anger, although I know it is really hard at first! But it is time to talk it out. Be your authentic self. Be transparent with yourself and with your spouse.

Own Only Your Feelings and Responsibilities
It is not sustainable for you to take on everyone else's responsibilities, emotions, and expectations. You can only keep everyone else happy for so long before one of the plates you've been balancing shatters into a million pieces. Furthermore, when

you keep peace at all costs, it can prevent other people from becoming responsible for their own behavior and feelings.

Maybe God is allowing your spouse to feel fragile and empty so he or she will run to God. The goal here is holiness, not perpetual happiness.

Set Healthy Boundaries
Did you know others will base their treatment of you on how you treat yourself? Decide what you can and can't do. Say "no" when necessary. Don't be pressured into doing things that are not sustainable long term or that make you feel uncomfortable.

Boundaries need to not only be set with each other but also with your children. Many couples unsuspectingly allow their kids to tear their relationship apart by giving in to their constant needs and ultimately dictating the tone of their marriage. Children need to know that mom and dad's relationship comes first, otherwise you may end up with a child-centered home instead of a Christ-centered home.

For some of you, this may sound scary or even unchristian. Perhaps you have no idea how to even begin to detach from your false thinking. Saying "no" and setting boundaries seems selfish. Assertiveness feels rude, or even harsh. In fact, you feel guilty for having an opinion that is different from those around you. But this type of mindset is unsustainable. Believe me, I know first-hand.

Set Biblical Priorities

God, marriage, family, and job—this is the biblical order. It is important to please God first. Find out who you are in Christ and base your worth on what God says about you. Your relationship with God is the foundation for all other relationships. The second priority is your marriage, not your job, or even your kids.

This is not always easy. Our kids can be demanding and so can our jobs. But it is so important to set aside time to talk with your spouse each day. Set boundaries with the kids. Have them go play while you and your spouse catch up from the day. You can call it "couch time." And give consequences for disruptions—it is that important. Learn how to maintain healthy relationship patterns with those around you so they don't drain your marriage.

Let go

A healthy marriage experiences both conflict and forgiveness. There are going to be times when your spouse is angry with you. Mentally decide you can live without that approval before the time comes. When it does happen, keep telling yourself you are okay. Release your spouse to God and let go.

If there is never conflict in your relationship, one of you is not being your authentic self. Real peace is not the absence of conflict, although that is a nice feeling. God's peace is what comes in the midst of a difficult situation; it is an inner rest. No matter how bad it looks on the outside, you can trust God with the details.

Know the Truth

Know who you are as a believer in Christ. It takes time to delve into scripture and find out who you are according to God. Here are some biblically based mantras to help realign your thinking. These mantras specifically deal with the lies of feeling worthless, powerless, and unloved. Unlike many self-help books, who rely on what we can do, these words of affirmation go back to our true source of help, God.

- God is good; I can trust Him (Lam. 3:25).
- I am capable of accomplishing good things through Christ whether or not I get the approval of others (Phil. 4:13).
- I am completely and wholly loved by God (Rom. 8:35).
- I can show up and act like an adult, putting away childish things (1 Cor. 13:11).
- Mistakes don't affect my worth (and I can even laugh at them) (Luke 12:7).
- What I say is important and worth hearing (Ps. 139:14).
- My value is based on what God says about me (Eph. 2:10).
- I can always depend on God no matter how bad it looks (2 Tim. 1:7).
- I can take ownership of my behavior (Gal. 2:20).

- I have the power to change with the help of the Holy Spirit (John 14:26).

- I am valued just as much as anyone else (Eph. 2:4–9).

- Everyone doesn't have to like me (1 Sam. 16:7).

- I can be content with who I am, knowing that I am a work in progress (2 Cor. 12:10).

- I have the power to make goals and dreams come true with God's help (Josh. 1:9).

- I can know others and be known (1 John 4:7).

LIVING LOVED

If you want to change, it is important to understand that God loves you. Believe it, internalize it, bask in it. Otherwise, this truth will sit in your Bible with no power.

It is time to start living loved. Refuse to wallow in shame. That temptation is from the pit of hell. Literally.

If you get nothing else from this book, please pay attention to this: I could not love others well, especially my spouse, until I accepted God's love for me first. I had to put away my pride and accept that God loved me, a broken sinner, just as much as everyone else.

Everything changed once I killed my pride and accepted that God loves me. It changed my negative attitude, removed my fear of rejection, helped me combat the lies, negated the self-pity, enabled me to stop the people-pleasing, and allowed me to trust again. Do I do this perfectly all the time? No, but I can celebrate the work God has done in my heart since I started this process.

What would your life look like if you believed God and lived loved every day? Or you looked at your worth through God's eyes? If you regularly told yourself how much you are loved by God and you are not powerless because you have the Holy Spirit guiding you?

I realize that for some of you, changing your mindset is not just difficult, it is terrifying. You may be thinking, "What if this doesn't work for me? What if I don't ever experience God's love personally? What if I never believe my worth is based on what God says?" "What if my situation never changes?" I dare you to try. Ask God to show you His extravagant love so you no longer crave the approval of others.

If you are struggling to find your worth, you may need to backtrack. Perhaps you need to address the lies you believe about yourself and others.

REFLECTION

1. Are you caught in a pattern of people-pleasing, anger, or withdrawal when relating to your spouse? How does it happen?

2. What scriptures point to your value as a person loved by God?

3. What are your priorities? List them in order.

4. In what ways can you be your authentic self? List them.

5. Will you embrace God's love and live loved? How will you do this?

CHAPTER REVIEW

1. Your spouse was never made to meet all your needs.

2. Show others how to treat you by treating yourself well.

3. Being emotionally vulnerable helps you become one with your spouse.

4. Accept that God loves you so you can love others well.

VERSES FOR SPIRITUAL WARFARE

Galatians 1:10

"Am I now trying to win the approval of human beings, or of God? Or am I trying to please people? If I were still trying to please people, I would not be a servant of Christ."

PRAYER

God, I ask You to help me clearly understand how valuable I am to You. That my worth is not based on what other people say (especially my spouse), but what You say about me. May my eyes be opened to all the scriptures that point to Your lavish love for me. I pray I would not fear man but fear You and trust You. Show me how to be honest with my spouse so that I am authentically known. Help my spouse to do the same with me. Keep us from withdrawing, exploding, or isolating from each other. When I feel vulnerable, let me run back to You for safety. Reveal to me how to keep my priorities in order, with You being first. Help me not to put other things before my spouse, such as kids, work, or social activities. I pray we would not be complacent but would intentionally make time for each other every day, so we stay unified. Give me the courage to set healthy boundaries and not feel guilty for saying "no" to things You don't want me to do.

CHAPTER 9

Liar, Liar, Pants on Fire

"Once our minds are 'tattooed' with negative thinking, our chances for long-term success diminish."

—John C. Maxwell,
Developing the Leader Within You

Early one morning, Andy and my teenager were eating breakfast together. I was still in bed, which made it a prime time for this child to vent about me. Whatever rules we had put in place were a thorn in this teen's flesh. To make matters worse, I had a reputation for ruining said child's fun on a regular basis with my negativity.

After listening for a good ten minutes, Andy simply said: "You know, the difference between mom and me is that I see the glass as half full, while she sees the glass as half empty. And … what's left is poison." They both started laughing. This one line diffused the whole situation.

As I dragged into the kitchen that morning, unsuspectingly the object of their laughter, I listened to what Andy had said about me. At first, I was a little miffed. And then I laughed too. It was pretty funny and also kind of true. I was Negative Nelly. My negativity from unresolved issues was affecting not only our marriage but also our kids. I seriously needed to get some help; it was time to find another counselor.

Truthfully, I had fought going to counseling because I didn't want to put in the necessary work. Why bring up deep hurts and open old wounds? It sounded like painful, time-consuming, dirty work. The past was over, done, kaput.

I was still clinging to the idea that God would magically erase all the issues from long ago and deliver me from my problems (without me having to do any work). I thought being a Christian automatically made me emotionally healthy. What I didn't realize is that I was skipping over the process of sanctification. God wanted me to look at myself in the mirror and be honest about my feelings. More importantly, He wanted me to confess my sins and deal with the idols in my life.

I wanted miracles. Deliverance. Magic. God wanted my heart. Every. Piece. Of. It. And for me to quit blaming everyone else.

While God still does perform miracles, it took awhile to realize I was going to have to face my demons head-on to get healing. This wasn't going away. I would need to feel the pain of the past and allow God to bind the broken places. Lysa TerKeurst (*It's Not Supposed to Be This Way*) says:

> Feeling the pain is the first step toward healing the pain. The longer we avoid the feeling, the more we delay our healing. We can numb it, ignore it, or pretend it doesn't exist, but all those options lead to an eventual breakdown, not a breakthrough. (page 36)

The first week in counseling, the new counselor asked me to go back to the beginning. What had happened to make me have such a low self-esteem? Sitting in her office that day, I remembered some very real hurts that shaped my thinking as a young child.

The family break with my grandparents was a primary one, but there were other incidents that contributed to my low opinion of myself. Difficult interactions at home, confusion about God, and how I fit in socially at school were just a few. Unforgiveness, pride, revenge, and anger were strongholds in my family, and sadly, they continued to manifest themselves even after our family's conversion to Christianity. Those sins, at times, seemed more powerful than the gospel of Jesus Christ.

This alone would have been enough to warrant many visits to a counselor's office, but there were other difficult events that reinforced my faulty thinking.

One of my most difficult memories had to do with my birth order. I was the youngest of three girls. There were many advantages to being the youngest child, but when you trail after two beautiful, smart, and sweet sisters, it's not so great.

Let me explain.

Both of my sisters were extroverted and pretty. They were both repeatedly on the high school homecoming court, both homecoming queens, both voted most popular, straight "A" students, and both captains of their cheer squad. My middle sister even won homecoming queen and captain of the cheer squad her junior year, not her senior year. This means she beat out all the senior girls in both areas. She then changed schools for her senior year (to a bigger school) and was nominated to be on the homecoming court as a new student at a new school. Who even does that?

I, on the other hand, was lanky and uncoordinated. I also had vision problems and wore glasses. While I had my fair share of academic accolades, I ended up being a late bloomer. I tried out for cheer my freshman year and didn't make it. Too gawky.

I was thankful to make the cheer squad my sophomore and junior years, but afterward I was named "most improved." Why they even give out that award is beyond me. After stewing over the award for a couple of days, I decided it was actually funny. My friends and I joked about it; it was no secret I was lacking in skills. Obviously, cheer captain was never in the cards for me. At least I had a sense of humor about the whole thing.

I tried basketball but broke my ankle the first part of the season my freshman year. The next thing was volleyball. I played for three years but never could perfect my overhand serve. I spent a lot of time warming the bench.

As you might guess, I never made it on the homecoming court. I was overlooked time and time again, which was painful. In my mind, I expected to be everything my sisters had been. Maybe even more. But it never happened.

All of this reinforced the belief that I didn't belong in my family and that I wasn't enough. Again, God kept whispering in my ear: precious, redeemed, enough, saved, beautiful, chosen. But I didn't believe it.

Perhaps you perpetuate some of the same lies in your own mind. You feel you are not enough or that you have been overlooked time and time again. You are not alone.

I recently asked women on Facebook to tell me the lies they have believed about themselves over the years. To my shock, I got a huge response. Let me share some of the things they said:

- I am not a good enough wife because I don't cook enough, clean enough, study the Bible enough, work out enough, serve enough, not bubbly enough, etc. I basically put such high standards on myself that no human can actually achieve. I also tend to subconsciously do this with God. I believe I have to check some list of unachievable requirements in order to be considered a "good Christian."
- Lie number one, love is tied to physical appearance. Lie number two, keeping struggles to myself protects my family from being affected.
- I have foolishly believed that feeling loved was connected to what I do for others. I *must* please them in order for them to have a relationship with me. If they didn't want a relationship, or if they rejected me, it must be my fault.
- I continue to struggle with the lie that I fail in all my various relationships if I say "no" to someone. It's difficult to say "no" to your spouse, parent, children, siblings, friends, and church family when they need help. But God has reminded me many times, it's not my job

(because I can't possibly be everywhere) to say "yes" every time.
- Fat all my life, need a nose and chin job, too tall, feet too big ... battled body dysmorphic disorder, low self-worth, shame, guilt all my life. (This came from the person who won Homecoming Queen at my high school.)
- That I matter less because I am a housewife and don't work outside the home ...

When I read those shame-filled thoughts, my heart broke. Then I looked at who wrote the posts. I knew these people. They weren't strangers; they were friends and family. People I loved. Some of the comments were from people I'd gone to school with over 40 years ago. How could this be? I never knew they struggled this deeply until they admitted it on my Facebook page.

That's what happens when we don't talk about it. Lies and shame stay in the dark and grow like a toxic mold, eating at us one spore at a time, until one day we have inhaled our own garbage for so long that we are completely overtaken by the lies and can't breathe God's Word into our lungs.

For a moment, I realized that God must feel heartbroken when He sees this happen to us. He hurts for us the same way I hurt for my beloved friends and family. We repeat these horrible phrases to ourselves (phrases we would never say to anyone else)—worthless, ugly, not enough, a failure, powerless, and unloved. While God says differently—loved, redeemed, beautiful, courageous, warrior, child of the Most High God. But we won't believe Him.

Why do we do this to ourselves? Why do we struggle with the truth? Last I checked, trashing other people never made them change, so why would trashing ourselves make us better?

It's not logical at all. It's emotional. And, ultimately, it's spiritual. It's a battle of the mind. Actually, it's a war. A very *big* war. And it started in the garden of Eden when Satan told Eve the first lie.

This is the single thing that has caused me the most heartache—believing and internalizing lies. I couldn't accept that I was unconditionally loved by God. I knew He loved everyone else, just not me. Because of this, I self-sabotaged. Looking back, I think shame fed the lies, and pride kept me from fully embracing the whole truth.

Something had to change.

During my 16 months in counseling, I realized just how harmful my thought patterns were. I put a stake in the ground. If I was going to live a full life, I needed to address the lies that had corrupted my mind.

Here is what I did (and still do) to defeat the lies. If this worked for me, I believe it can work for you too. Most of all, realize that you cannot do this without God's help. It is about surrendering your will and giving God authority over your thought life.

HOW TO STOP THE LIES

Ask God to show you the lies.
Pray and ask God to show you the lies you believe about yourself, others, or even Him. Many times, we are blinded by our own version of truth, and we don't see what God thinks about us or our situation.

Acknowledge what you are doing is wrong.
Lying to yourself (or to others) is a sin. Admit you have an issue with believing Satan over God, and it is producing death instead of life. By the way, did you know Satan's name means "accuser." He is accusing you with lies day and night!

Make the commitment to change.
If you want to stop believing the lies in your head, you must be committed to changing your behavior, even when it feels like it is not working or it hurts too much to keep going.

You can't change your thought patterns quickly. You are literally entrenching new neuropathways in your brain that have never been there before and, at the same time, abandoning the old pathways.

Combat each lie with scripture.
On a piece of paper, write down every lie you believe about yourself. Truthfully, this is kind of fun to do. You are calling out Satan and telling him he has been caught; it is your chance to "write" your wrongs.

Next, get note cards and address every lie with scripture. If you need help, search the web using the keyword "scriptures about _____." Example topics: trusting God, His love, forgiveness, worth, anger, etc. It will give you relevant scriptures about your particular subject. Click on the verse and copy it onto a note card.

Put one or two Bible verses on each note card to combat every lie you have believed. Then throw away the paper with the lies on it. You can rip it up or even have a ceremony and burn it. (If you want free scripture note cards, go to momremade.com and click on "Free Printables." You can download them right now if you don't want to make your own.)

Read every day.
Start reading the note cards every day without fail. Pray the verses. Put your name in them where appropriate to personalize them. Read them out loud so you hear them too. When you do this, you are creating those new neuropathways in your brain and abandoning the old thought patterns you used to have.

Let me be clear—you are actively reprogramming your mind. Therefore, it's important to also protect your mind from garbage in bad movies, trashy books, music, or any other materials that are not godly. Those are counterproductive. In fact, they feed the monster. Input equals output.

Choose to believe.

This next phase takes great faith. Simply believe God even if you don't feel it. This is about a choice, not a feeling. Feelings come later. Way later!

It is time to choose to believe you are loved. You are precious in God's sight. He has a good plan for you. Internalize those truths, even if you don't feel them immediately. "Then you will know the truth, and the truth will set you free" (John 8:32).

Jesus said, "I am . . . the truth" (John 14:6). He is the very personification of truth. When we choose to believe Satan's lies, we are quite literally rejecting Jesus Christ Himself. That thought makes it easier for me to reject the lies.

Making the Change

If you want to change a behavior, you will have to be vigilant to catch yourself when the lies creep in. It may take a few minutes before you realize what you are doing in those moments, so give yourself grace.

Once you catch yourself in a lying thought, visualize a big, red stop sign. The red color should trigger the thought, "Danger! Stop it! Now!" Then consciously interrupt your thoughts with something God says about you or your situation. Going forward you have the choice to consciously continue with the lies (wallow) or stop the lies and replace them with the truth. (Hint: Wallowing is not the right choice.)

When the Lies Pop Up

Lies creep in without notice, just like they did in the garden of Eden when Adam and Eve sinned. They rear their ugly heads when you are tired, upset with others, feel rejected or angry, or when you feel God has done you wrong. They especially come when flashbacks from past hurts hit your mind at the most unsuspecting moments and you wonder why God didn't intercede right then.

Satan is going to tell you that repeating God's Word over and over in your mind isn't going to work. I am here to tell you it does work. God's Word has incredible power, which is why Satan is going to work overtime on you to convince you otherwise. So, when you are weary and the spiritual warfare comes, be ready for it. (FYI: It's coming.) Rebuke the devil and tell him to flee if the spirit of oppression and lies won't leave you. When you feel as if God is silent, remember He is still working. Don't give in to your feelings!

My life was interrupted by a God who loved me enough to let me suffer. Not just a little. He allowed me to suffer a whole lot so eventually I would be broken enough to change my thinking and come to the truth. My prayer is you find wholeness and start believing the truth too. God wants you to give Him complete control of your thought life.

If you are struggling to let go of those bad tapes in your head, it may mean you need to forgive those who hurt you first. Forgiveness is not easy, but it is an integral part of your journey to wholeness.

REFLECTION

1. What lies do you believe about yourself?
2. What lies have others spoken about you?
3. How have you been dealing with these lies?
4. What is the truth about you?
5. Are you willing to combat the lies with Scripture, starting today?

CHAPTER REVIEW

1. Sometimes God allows suffering to get our attention so we will change our behavior.
2. Scripture is the best way to reprogram your thinking.
3. Choose to believe truth even when you don't feel it.
4. Spiritual warfare is real, and you will experience it when you start speaking the truth.

VERSES FOR SPIRITUAL WARFARE

John 8:32

"Then you will know the truth, and the truth will set you free."

1 John 1:6

"If we claim to have fellowship with him and yet walk in the darkness, we lie and do not live out the truth."

PRAYER

God, help me to remember You are not only the author of truth, but You are also the Truth. When I choose to believe lies, I am really choosing to reject You. When I am tempted to get lazy and succumb to old ways of thinking, redirect my thoughts back to You. Thank You for giving me the strength to address the lies head-on and discipline my mind to think only what is true, holy, pure, righteous, and good. Grant me the resolve to write Your words down and meditate on them every day until biblical thought patterns are entrenched in my brain. When I become weary and don't believe what You say, help me to stand on faith alone until Your words are second nature. When lies are spoken to me, help me to recognize and reject them. Help me to stand firm on Your words no matter what is going on around me.

CHAPTER 10

Forgiving the Unforgettable

"The ultimate proof of total forgiveness takes place when we sincerely petition the Father to let those who have hurt us off the hook—even if they have hurt not only us, but also those close to us."

—R.T. Kendall,
Total Forgiveness

We had only been married a year when we bought our first house. Don't get too impressed—it was a fixer-upper in every way possible. Truthfully, we had no idea what we were getting into, and it showed. We definitely bought the worst house on the block, like all the HGTV remodeling pros suggested. In my mind, remodeling was going to be like a tidy 30-minute program, not an all-out assault on my marriage with a huge opportunity to forgive.

For starters, Andy had a full-time job. He could only work on the house at night and on the weekends, unlike the superstar renovators who get everything done in a weekend. I must admit, having an accountant for a husband who is also handy is great. You save lots of money. But it also means he alone is going to fix everything, even if it takes years.

One Friday night, Andy told me he hired some help for the next morning. They were going to rip off the peeling sheetrock in our son's bedroom and install beautiful new walls in the afternoon. I was a little skeptical about the whole thing, but Andy reassured me our newborn son would be back in his bed by nighttime with very little mess. He said, and I quote, "Slit, slit, out the window."

He would cut the sheetrock and then slide it out the window. Nothing would go through the house. No fuss, no mess. It sounded awesome. I agreed to the extra help because I was ready to speed things up.

Sure enough, bright and early Saturday morning a group of Kurdish refugee men Andy knew from church showed up at our door. They were ready and willing to work. Excitedly, I got our son out of bed and grabbed his clothes, a few toys, and some diapers. I hurried out of his room with great expectations. I couldn't wait to see the reveal that evening.

Here I was, the star of my own home makeover show. I could see it now: "Oh, my goodness. Ahhh! It's so beautiful. I just want to thank all of you who worked so hard to make this happen in one day. You are amazing." Then I would shower Andy with hugs and kisses. It was going to be great.

Okay, back to reality. As I was standing in the den, I saw Andy enter our son's bedroom. He looked back at me and told me not to come in so the dust would stay contained in one room. Dust? What dust? I had gone to great lengths to decorate my son's bedroom and didn't want it messed up. Again, he assured me, "Slit, slit, out the window."

Andy is the eternal optimist. My tendency to be Negative Nelly is my way of swinging him back to reality. I ignored my gut and hoped for the best. A little while later, I saw Andy sheepishly walk to the garage and come back with a chainsaw. A chainsaw!

Without a word, he disappeared behind my son's bedroom door again and ripped the pull cord. That's when the noise started. *Reeeee, rrrreeeee, vroooom!* I hadn't realized the "slitting" would be with a chainsaw. My husband used that chainsaw in my baby's bedroom to cut up the walls. By the way, nothing got covered beforehand.

You can imagine my horror as I listened on the other side of those closed doors. I was not going to be the star of an HGTV show. No, I was the star of the *Texas Chainsaw Massacre*. Soon after, I smelled exhaust fumes and saw a fine white powder billowing up from under my son's door. It rested in every nook and cranny like newly fallen snow. Panicked, I quickly took our son outside so we wouldn't inhale the exhaust fumes or the "snow."

When they were all done, the men came outside into the fresh air. Like toy soldiers, they filed out one by one, each looking funnier than the last. They were completely covered in white powder with only the flesh around their eyes showing their natural skin color. Andy included. They looked like they had been rolled in flour, like pieces of chicken ready to be fried.

I was trying to contain my laughter. These poor men had no idea what they had gotten themselves into that day. I seriously hoped Andy would be generous. Hazard pay, perhaps? That's when it hit me—my house! Oh, gosh.

I ran inside and saw it looked very similar to the men standing outside. All of the furniture was covered in a thick layer of white dust. The dust did not stay contained in the bedroom. Our Christmas tree (it was December), which was not flocked, had a complimentary dusting of white snow, along with the rest of the furniture and decorations around the house. Not to mention my son's room, which was not only white but missing sheetrock.

Needless to say, that was the last day we spent in our home for a good month. Unfortunately, it took that long to get the walls back up, texture, and paint the bedroom. Oh, and clean up the "snow." I was no longer the star of *Extreme Makeover: Home Edition*. In fact, I was homeless. And the inside of my house looked like Frosty the Snowman had exploded.

Thank goodness my parents took us in. But we missed the first Christmas in our new home. I was resentful. No, I was furious. Andy and I barely talked to each other during that Christmas holiday. Down deep, I knew Andy was trying to make a home for us. But getting there was not easy. Those early remodeling years tried our marriage like nobody's business. As much as I wanted to forgive him, I struggled to let go of this major disruption. It took time to learn it was better to work together than hold a grudge.

LEARNING TO FORGIVE YOUR SPOUSE

Unforgiveness is a trap. At the end of the day, not forgiving will destroy you as a person. It will destroy your marriage and your family. You can blame marital conflict on any number of things, but in the end, a lack of forgiveness is often the nail in the coffin.

For me, the habit of unforgiveness started years before I said, "I do." Add this habit to my diet of lies and people-pleasing, and I was certainly not set up for marital bliss. It took a long time for me to realize that my refusal to forgive family was the main source of tension in my life. That's why I am telling you to choose to forgive now; it will save you a lot of trouble in your marriage.

No matter what has happened or how bad the offense, unforgiveness will eat you alive. You have to let God into the equation. Some of you are bristling right now: "Julie, you have no idea what I have gone through." You're right, I don't. But God does. If you are a follower of Jesus, He says to forgive. There are no exceptions. Believe me, from one unforgiver to another, I have looked in the Bible ad nauseum. Those exceptions are not there.

WHAT ABOUT JUSTICE?

I know forgiveness seems unfair. Actually, it is unfair. That is the point. But if you are demanding fairness with others, then you must accept the same justice system for yourself. Ultimately, that line of thinking leads to hell, because that is what we all truly deserve.

I know it is hard to let go of hurts and allow God to administer justice in His time because we may never see the scales balanced. But that is not our business. It's God's business.

Perhaps it feels like forgiving someone means whatever happened was "not that big of a deal" or that whatever you experienced "wasn't that bad." This is not true. God knows how much you hurt. He sees it all, and, in fact, He hurts with you deeply. He has not overlooked the sins against you.

As an innocent, wounded person, you may feel righteous in your desire for retribution. I get that. It's natural to want wrongs to be righted. Who doesn't? So, let's just say you do see justice carried out. What does this actually look like? What do you want from your spouse or others, besides an apology? Money sometimes helps, but then what? An equal amount of suffering or public embarrassment? And exactly how much is enough? When is that debt paid in full?

If you follow this line of thinking, you will never be satisfied. Furthermore, no matter what you get in return, it will never help you recover what you have lost. So, stop trying. It will not bring you joy. Real forgiveness releases the debtor(s) from the obligation of paying the debt they owe. It may even mean we step in and pay the debt the other person owes us. (This is different from enabling.)

What you can do instead is grieve the real loss. Additionally, you can start praying for change. Genuine heart change. Acknowledge what was taken from you and allow God to cover you with His balm of healing. Ask Him to make it right.

When you release your offenses to God, He will bring about justice. He will eventually make all things right. Your own recovery may look different from what you think, but God is creative. He redeems what the locusts have eaten when we give Him our pile of rubble (Joel 2:25).

Truthfully, only God has all the facts and can rightly judge the situation. When you let the offender off your hook, you are releasing him or her onto God's hook. Do you really want to be on the other end of God's hook? I don't.

God is a righteous judge who may tarry due to His mercy, but He will not forget. While it is hard to wait, we must trust that His timing is perfect. So, step back and let Him work His justice. Give up your futile attempts to right the scales.

As a sidenote, I want to emphasize that in this book I am focusing on offenses that are not worthy of a court appearance. They are still hurtful—like dirty muffins and chainsaws—but they are not criminal. If a crime has been committed against you, it is imperative that you report it. Ignoring evil will only breed more evil. Forgiveness is still the end goal, no matter what has happened, but you must take appropriate steps to report a criminal offense. Secondly, please take measures to ensure the safety of you and your loved ones.

WHAT ABOUT REVENGE?

Like me, you may be tempted to recover what was lost through revenge. The Bible says vengeance belongs to God. Is it our right to rob God and take what rightfully belongs to Him?

Nowhere in the Bible does it say that vengeance belongs to man. Consult Romans 12:19, Hebrews 10:30, Deuteronomy 32:35, Psalm 94, and Isaiah 63:4.

Justice is given by those who are impartial, while vengeance is unfairly handed out by the offended, who is never impartial, and is often bitter.

R.T. Kendall in *Total Forgiveness* says,

> How can we be sure that there is no bitterness left in our hearts? Bitterness is gone when there is no desire to get even with or punish the offender, when I do or say nothing that would hurt his reputation or future and when I truly wish him well in all he seeks to do. (page 43)

God knows we will never be fair when we play judge and jury in our own cases. No court of law would ever allow the prosecutor to also be the judge or juror. Yet, this is what we do when we try to punish our offenders.

The outcome is up to God. Whatever happens, it is not our place to manipulate the situation or seek retribution for our pain. Matthew 5:39 says:

> simply ignore insignificant insults or trivial losses and do not bother to retaliate—maintain your dignity, your self-respect, your poise. (AMP)

Forgiveness doesn't mean we release our need for good boundaries. We just release our right to retaliate. And don't forget, when you retaliate against your spouse, you are also hurting yourself because you are united as one.

FORGIVING OURSELVES

The most painful sins in my own life have been those I repeated due to my unforgiving spirit. My bitterness caused me to fall into the same traps again and again. Part of the remedy has been not only to forgive others but also to forgive myself. I allowed grace into my life. Once I did this, the doorway opened for the Holy Spirit to enter the situation and begin healing all the raw places.

R.T. Kendall continues:

> It is almost impossible to say which comes first—forgiving others so you will be able to forgive yourself or forgiving yourself so you will be able to forgive others. But it is not total forgiveness until both are equally true. (page 153)

Once I let myself off the hook, I was free to be used by God. I felt a release to be honest about my struggles and not feel shameful. Forgiving myself has released me to be the person I was intended to be in the first place. I am able to help others instead of being bogged down with my own junk.

FORGIVING GOD

First of all, God doesn't need forgiving because He doesn't sin. But sometimes we need to work through what we don't understand about God. When He didn't intervene on my behalf and magically adjust Andy's job situation, heal my colon, and fix my family hurts, I was angry. I wanted peace in my marriage, in my family, and I wanted physical healing. I was frustrated with God for not providing it in my time frame. Unfortunately, my worldview was not biblical.

As a rule-follower, I expected God to give justice to those who had hurt me. I demanded He strike them with lightning bolts. In fact, I prayed for that to happen! When it didn't happen, I saw God as weak, uncaring, feckless, and distant. A God who would not or could not rescue me. When God didn't vindicate me in my own time or play by my rules, I concluded He didn't love me.

Loving words written in the Bible rolled off my back and hit the ground with a loud thud. I didn't have a full understanding of what He was doing, so I assumed the worst. I lacked trust in His goodness. Maybe He was good to others, but He was not good to me, nor did He love me.

I was angry He allowed so many issues in my life to collide at one time. He could have stopped these interruptions, yet He didn't. Why? In my heart, I knew I could manage things better than God if He would just let me have my way. I wanted control, but every time I made a power grab, my circumstances seemed to worsen. Clearly, God needed to work in my heart.

I could not see what He saw. I could not see His goodness or His love in the midst of my suffering.

IS FORGIVENESS BIBLICAL?

We expect God to forgive us for our sins against Him, but He, in turn, asks us to forgive each other in the same way.

"For if you forgive other people when they sin against you, your heavenly Father will also forgive you. But if you do not forgive others their sins, your Father will not forgive your sins" (Matthew 6:14–15).

I would also refer you to the story of the wicked servant in Matthew 18:21–35. He was forgiven a large debt by his master but was unwilling to forgive the much smaller debt of a fellow servant. When the master heard of his actions, the wicked servant was put in jail. The application for us: God expects us to forgive the smaller debts of our fellow men since He has already forgiven us for such a large debt—our sin against a holy God.

When we don't forgive, we put ourselves in jail. We are imprisoned by our own unforgiving hearts and are no longer free. Ironically, we are the only ones who have the key to set ourselves free. We must decide to unlock the door and walk away from the anger and bitterness. No one else can do it for us.

It's hard to forgive and set necessary boundaries all at once. This is a very delicate balance, since many of us bounce between extremes—an explosive temper, stuffed emotions, or withdrawal. I keep coming back to 1 Corinthians 13:4–5:

> Love is patient, love is kind. It does not envy, it does not boast, it is not proud. It does not dishonor others, it is not self-seeking, it is not easily angered, it keeps no record of wrongs.

Someday, I want to look at Jesus face to face and say that I have done everything I can to forgive everyone for everything. I don't want to do the bare minimum. How about you? Are you living in complete obedience to His words?

WHAT IS REAL FORGIVENESS?

Forgiveness is freely given; it is not earned. It is also not a feeling. It is something we choose to do. Many times, the feelings come later. So, if you are waiting for this overwhelming urge to "let it all go," you may be waiting a long time. It doesn't always work that way.

Sometimes forgiveness is just a decision and then a process that works itself out over time. I have found the deeper the hurt, the longer it takes to completely forgive.

Lysa TerKeurst says:

> As my counselor has explained to me, your decision to forgive the facts of what happened is done in a specific moment in time. But the process of working through all the emotions from the impact of what happened will likely happen over time. (*Forgiving What You Can't Forget*, pages 49–51)

Total forgiveness means releasing the offenders of any wrongdoing, even if they never admit they are wrong or there is never reconciliation. In fact, you blame them for nothing and forgive them for everything. It doesn't mean we pretend we are not hurt, cover it up, repress feelings, or stay in denial. Real forgiveness means we are fully aware of what happened—every painful detail—and we still choose to let it go.

We can't humanly forget the offenses, but we can choose not to dwell on them. This is real forgiveness, just like God does for us. He chooses not to remember our sin, even though He knows every last painful detail of what we have done against Him.

June Hunt, counselor and founder of Hope for the Heart, has written these go-to statements in her book *Anger: Facing the Fire Within*. They help us understand how to release our rights regarding an offense:

- Release your right to hear "I'm sorry" for the offense.
- Release your right to dwell on the offense.
- Release your right to hold on to the offense.
- Release your right to keep bringing up the offense (page 59)

These instructions are not easy to carry out, but I have found them helpful when I am struggling to release difficult situations that include people who aren't sorry. Or perhaps they have even passed away.

Another thing you can do is pray. Praying for those who hurt you is one behavior that sets Christians apart from the world. Can you pray for God to prosper them, keep them safe, and for God to forgive them for what they have done to you? It also won't hurt to pray for their repentance and for mercy in their lives too. Jesus is the ultimate example for us. He prayed these very things while hanging on the cross (Luke 23:34). If He did it, we can follow after Him.

This is all hard. It might even sound outrageous. However, the power of darkness has fallen away from my life since I have made it a practice to forgive and pray for my offenders. Satan no longer has a grip on me, my health, my family relationships, or my marriage. I am free.

Embracing forgiveness has helped me to love my husband like never before. In fact, I am crazy in love with him after 30 years of marriage. How often do you hear that?

WHAT IS RECONCILIATION?

Reconciliation is different from forgiveness. In her same book, *Anger: Facing the Fire Within,* June Hunt reminds us: "Forgiveness focuses on the offense whereas reconciliation focuses on the relationship" (page 63).

Biblical reconciliation is when two people, who are willing to admit wrongs, decide to work together to repair the relationship. There is a sustained effort and real change. A healthy reconciliation is not forced, coerced, or manipulated. More importantly, trust is earned over time. It comes slowly. You cannot reconcile with someone who is not willing to change or who is not repentant.

God's perfect will is for couples to reconcile—often. My pastor frequently says, "A happy marriage is the union of two very good forgivers." This is so true! It takes work, but it is possible when two people are committed to the relationship.

Unfortunately, there are times when trust has been so fractured that there is nothing left to build on. When this happens, reconciliation can be difficult, if not dangerous.

Some people just aren't safe, and there is nothing you can do to fix that. That doesn't mean you are off the hook. God commands us to forgive even when choosing not to remain in the same living space. Most of all, you can love from afar by praying. God desires unity, but it takes two people to be committed to this plan. Are you committed to doing your part and leaving the rest to God?

WHAT ABOUT ABUSE?

While this did not happen in my marriage, I do understand some of the nuances of abuse. Love doesn't mean staying in a relationship if the other party is abusive. Your spouse may not be trustworthy. You may have to love from afar.

If you have lived with an oppressor, you understand the cycle of apologies, gifts, and then more abuse, but no real repentance. This can't continue. In her book *Is It Abuse?* Darby R. Strickland says:

When an oppressor genuinely repents, he will be alarmed by his behavior. He will publicly confess it and commit to seeking expert help instead of trying to escape consequences. He will be afraid of his own capacity for evil and will weep for the damage that he had done—not for what he might lose (see Matt 18:8–9). He will do whatever it takes to make his wife comfortable. He will be eager to make amends and will refrain from pressuring his wife to forgive him. (page 139)

FORGIVENESS AND YOUR MARRIAGE

As I have said before, we often bring baggage into marriage. I found that looking back at my family history helped me recognize why I often reacted the way I did.

Personally, my anger stemmed from old offenses left unforgiven. I had to take the time to go back and address those hurts completely before I found relief.

While many things were not my fault, I was still responsible for how I filed it into my memory, processed the emotions, and acted on them. Truly, I suffered with self-righteousness and self-protection, both rooted in pride. Like Adam, I wanted to blame others including God, so I didn't have to take responsibility for my actions.

If you have a stronghold of unforgiveness in your life, take time to consider what led to that pattern. It may have started long before your spouse ever entered the picture.

Chances are you are dealing with some baggage, perhaps from things that happened long ago, before you were even married. It is not healthy to continually obsess over what happened to you, but there is a reason you are stuck. And the past may hold the key. Addressing the whole truth will help you to release what was done to you.

You can stop generational sins from continuing in your family line by surrendering them to God and clearing the slate. But it takes time and a willingness to let go.

SEEK HELP

It is unlikely you will be able to work through all of your issues alone if there are deep hurts. That's okay. In fact, it's better to seek wise advice. In my case, I needed a Christian counselor to help me walk through some difficult situations. I also did a Christian 12-step program called Re:generation. It helped me identify root issues (idols) I didn't realize were at work in my life.

I don't know what has happened in your marriage or your family. Maybe you don't really know either. My guess is that if you are reading this book, you need some encouragement and hope. The best thing Andy and I ever did was forgive. We stopped trying to change each other and instead worked on our own hearts. Over time, God brought us together as one because we quit focusing on the faults of the other person. Instead, we dealt with our own baggage.

When we did have conflict, we learned how to fight fairly using tools that foster respect and acknowledge dignity of the other person. Let me share some of those tools with you in the next chapter.

REFLECTION

1. Are you struggling with unforgiveness? What happened?
2. Do you want revenge instead of letting God bring justice?
3. In what ways do you struggle with forgiving yourself? With "forgiving" God?
4. In what situations do you struggle with self-righteousness?
5. Is God calling you to reconcile with your spouse? How?

CHAPTER REVIEW

1. Forgiveness is commanded by God.
2. Forgiveness doesn't mean what happened wasn't bad.
3. God will bring justice in His time and in His way.
4. Reconciliation is different from forgiveness.
5. It is possible to break the cycle of unforgiveness if you are willing to do the work.

VERSE FOR SPIRITUAL WARFARE

Matthew 6:14

"For if you forgive other people when they sin against you, your heavenly Father will also forgive you."

PRAYER

God, thank You for forgiving me when You died on the cross, even though I did not deserve it. Help me to remember this as I forgive others. I pray You would give me the same heart You have when dealing with offenses. Let me be the first to let it go, even when I don't feel like it. Help me speak blessings instead of curses as I am processing through the details. Wherever there has been separation, I pray for the balm of forgiveness to cover the matter, despite what has been said or done. Do not let revenge enter into the equation. Where there is sin against another, give all parties a heart of repentance. God, give me the strength to pray for those who have hurt me even though I may not feel like doing it. By faith, I ask for full reconciliation in cases where there is brokenness. If there is no repentance, help me to completely forgive the matter, trusting You with the full outcome. Protect my heart and give me wisdom as I move forward.

CHAPTER 11

The Mouse That Changed Our House

"Only by going vertical and surrendering your life daily to Christ will you find the ability to resolve conflict with your spouse."

—Dave and Ann Wilson,
Vertical Marriage

We had a cat named Patches. She was a hunter. In fact, we called her "Killer" half the time because she regularly brought offerings to our doorstep that were, well, shocking. Not to get too graphic, but by the time the critters ended up on our back porch, they were usually missing body parts.

Patches had a particular affinity for birds and mice (and rats if she got lucky). We lived near water so there were plenty of things to choose from. We often joked that one day she was going to drag a bobcat onto our doorstep. Frankly, we never knew what was on the menu from day to day.

One evening, Andy was home alone while I was at prayer group. As usual, he let the cat inside for the night before going to bed. Many times, when we called her to come in, she would run through the door with a dead thing in her mouth; it was a horrible problem we couldn't seem to control. On this particular night, the cat upped her game. She came running in with a mouse. And not a dead mouse, but a live mouse. I repeat. A live mouse.

When Andy saw what she had, he hollered after her. It must have startled her because she immediately opened her mouth and dropped the mouse. As soon as the mouse hit the floor, it ran off. It was nowhere to be found.

In Andy's defense, he claims he looked for the mouse for a long time. But he eventually gave up and went to bed with the mouse still on the loose. I came home refreshed from my night of praying and went to sleep happily, while the mouse did who knows what.

The next morning, we began our usual routine. We dressed, exercised, and ate breakfast. There was no mention of a mouse in the house. About 10 minutes before Andy was set to leave for work, he said, "Oh, last night, I let Patches in, and she had a mouse." I was waiting for the rest of the story, only nothing else was said.

Eventually, I asked, "Oh, did you get it?" Quietly, he admitted, "She dropped it." I didn't understand. Finally, he offered, "It was alive." I asked again, "So, did you get it?"

No answer.

And then I realized what he was saying. Immediately, I exploded: "There's a mouse in the house and you didn't tell me? I can't believe I slept all night with that thing running around. Are you kidding me? Did you not think to tell me before now?" He told me it was just an itty-bitty field mouse. No big deal. Except it was a big deal to me!

The Mouse That Changed Our House

That's when Andy got up, brushed his teeth, and left for work. He wasn't up for any drama I had planned. On his way out, he said he would catch it when he got home.

Meanwhile, I was thinking of ways to get rid of it *now*. I wanted that thing gone. After I killed the mouse, I was going to make sure Andy knew it was a "big deal."

Any and every spiritual thought I'd had the night before at prayer group went out the window. I did not think kindly of my husband, to say the least. What we had was a failure to communicate.

I was not staying in the house with that thing. Small field mouse or not, I was leaving. So, I ran out the door before I died of some random disease such as the bubonic plague. I ran errands, went to eat, and killed all the time I could. Eventually, I got tired and came home.

At the end of the day, I was worn out. I was tired of fighting Andy and the mouse in my mind. Before Andy came home, I decided to have a few words alone with the mouse. I sat in the kitchen near the wall where I thought it was hiding and quietly told the mouse it was not going to destroy my marriage, no matter how big or diseased it was.

And then it hit me. I realized I had a choice. I could either work with my husband to get rid of the darn thing, or I could continue to fight and blame him.

I had a choice about everything else too. Our marriage, my reactions, and our future as a couple. I had the power to make it good or bad. If I was going to make it good, I needed to act like an adult and quit with the antics. It was time to stop being a child and focusing on how Andy needed to change. The real question was, "What do I need to do to change?" First Corinthians 13:11 says:

> When I was a child, I talked like a child, I thought like a child, I reasoned like a child. When I became a man, I put the ways of childhood behind me.

That day I chose to put away childish things and work together with my husband as an adult. We would make the best out of a bad situation. Furthermore, I realized Andy wasn't even the problem. The mouse was the problem. This was just one more way I had let Satan get between us. The real enemy was Satan, not my husband.

Yes, I was angry he didn't tell me about the mouse sooner. And he apologized. Talking through it, Andy realized he wasn't married to himself. There were two people in the marriage, and one of them did not like mice, especially in the house. But there was nothing he could do to fix the problem at the moment. I would have to wait patiently for him to catch the mouse.

It took three days to find it, but eventually, Andy caught it like he said he would. In the meantime, we hopped around the house, constantly looking for a furry critter, paranoid there was something on our feet, all the while laughing about our predicament. And I showed up as an adult instead of pouting, giving the silent treatment, sighing loudly, walking away, slamming doors, eye-rolling, rude remarks, etc. I decided not to make the situation any worse than it was already.

In a way, that darn mouse woke me up to the truth. It was time to get aggressive and learn how to deal with conflict in a healthy way. I needed to address my faulty thinking: the people-pleasing, the lies I believed, and the unforgiveness from the past. My baggage was ruining the present and the future. It was time to approach all of our conflicts like an adult. I realized that it wasn't the conflict that was the sin, it was how I was handling it.

I needed to change my perspective. I had forgotten we were on the same team. We needed to work together against the problem, not each other. Talking about it was the healthiest way to bring us back to oneness.

HOW TO DEAL WITH CONFLICT

If you are struggling with how to deal with conflict, I suggest you use these skills when working through a difficult situation. These tips are rewritten in my own words after 30 years of marriage experience, but they are heavily inspired by three sources: Marriage CORE, re-engage, and marriage counseling. I believe these tips and reminders will help deescalate your situation and make it easier to achieve unity.

Before you approach your spouse, ask yourself what you may be doing to negatively affect the situation. Take ownership of your triggers.

The way you communicate has a big impact on the quality of your marriage. This means putting away childish behavior such as sarcasm, eye-rolling, yelling, tantrums, silent treatment, slamming doors, revenge, etc. Show up as an adult who has a kind and even tone.

You are not married to yourself. There are two people in the marriage with differing views, each equally important.

- Approach the conflict as two adults. Constantly remind yourself to put away childish responses and/or behaviors.
- As you discuss the problem, quietly pray for God to give you both humble hearts to work through the differences.
- Resist the urge to leave the room in the middle of a conversation or to withdraw and ignore your spouse.
- If you feel the situation escalating, communicate that you need a time-out. Take time to calm down before you lose your temper.
- Ask for a "redo." When you notice a conversation declining, ask to start over with a more appropriate attitude.
- Instead of negatively interpreting what your spouse is saying (colored by your own past experiences), listen and ask for clarification.
- You don't have to agree with your spouse, but it is important you respect, validate, and understand what your spouse is saying.
- Instead of people-pleasing, learn to honestly state your thoughts. If you are scared to express them, say so.

- Keep reminding each other that you are on the same team when you are in the middle of conflict. The goal is oneness.
- Remember that your spouse is not the enemy; Satan is the real enemy.
- Put your spouse's needs before yours.
- Forgive. Overlook minor offenses and extend grace.
- If possible, don't wait until the late evening to start a difficult discussion. It is hard to practice these tips when you are tired.
- Not everything can be resolved in an hour. With particularly hard situations, emphasize that you still love your spouse and ask for more time to pray and think through the problem. Agree to a time in the near future (within a day or so) to come back and talk.
- If you cannot resolve the conflict on your own, get help from a wise couple or pastor, join a marriage support group, or find a counselor.

Putting these guidelines in place will make it easier for each of you to feel safe when discussing a problem and finding a resolution. Over time, if you keep practicing these tips, you will get momentum in your ability to work together as a team. Keep reminding yourself that biblical unity is not "peace at all costs," but rather a balance of give-and-take from both sides.

IS YOUR MARRIAGE A COVENANT OR A CONTRACT?

Another issue that may be hindering conflict resolution is the commitment level you have with your spouse. Do you view your marriage as a covenant or a contract? Contractual love is love that is conditional and unreliable. It is tainted with selfish motivation. "If you do this . . . I will do that." If the conditions are not met, a favorable response is not given in return. This is what we *all* bring to the marriage without God.

Covenant love is different. It is unconditional love; it is deep, strong, and dependable no matter what happens. Furthermore, it can't be earned; it is freely given without conditions. This is the kind of love that makes a marriage work.

In the Bible, a covenant was made with the cutting and sealing of blood. In the Old Testament, it was made through circumcision. In the New Testament, Jesus made a new covenant by shedding His blood on the cross for us. God kept His side of the covenant, even when we couldn't keep our side.

Jesus is our best example for covenant love. While we may not have to die on a cross, He is asking us to die to our selfish motivations every single day. Luke 9:23 says:

> Then he said to them all: "Whoever wants to be my disciple must deny themselves and take up their cross daily and follow me."

The Mouse That Changed Our House

We have probably all experienced contractual love and covenant love at one time or another. There is no comparison between the two. Covenant love is, by far, the greatest love you can experience. But this is impossible without God's help. Ask God to give you new eyes for your spouse. That you would see him or her as a beloved child of God, worthy of covenant love, no matter how you feel. Choose to do the right thing, even if your spouse is not at the moment.

If you are frustrated because your feel your spouse's love is more conditional than covenant, perhaps it is time to get down to business and pull out the "big guns." The greatest thing you can do to change your spouse is also the most powerful weapon you have in your arsenal. What is this secret weapon you ask?

Prayer. (And, yes, it really works.)

REFLECTION

1. How are you and your spouse working together or against each other to resolve conflict?
2. In what ways will you communicate with each other more appropriately?
3. Are extreme emotions easily triggered in you? How is it affecting others?
4. How will you change your behavior and act like the adult in the relationship?
5. How do you view your relationship? Is it a covenant or a contract?

CHAPTER REVIEW

1. Your spouse is not your enemy. Satan is your enemy.
2. Triggers and extreme reactions point to unhealed wounds.
3. Show up as an adult in your marriage.
4. The conflict itself is not necessarily the problem. The way you handle the conflict can be the primary problem.
5. Covenant love is the kind of love that makes a marriage work.

THE MOUSE THAT CHANGED OUR HOUSE

VERSE FOR SPIRITUAL WARFARE

1 Peter 3:8–9

"Finally, all of you, be like-minded, be sympathetic, love one another, be compassionate and humble. Do not repay evil with evil or insult with insult. On the contrary, repay evil with blessing, because to this you were called so that you may inherit a blessing."

PRAYER

Thank You, God, for helping me to address the way I communicate with my spouse. When I am angry, remind me to be sympathetic, loving, compassionate, and humble. When I am triggered, help me to calm down and realize this is an unhealed wound from the past that needs Your touch. Give me the grace to overlook minor offenses even though I may be tempted to nitpick. Reveal any hidden sins in our lives that need to be addressed. Show us how to change our behaviors so we will be like-minded. Where we do not agree, help us to go back to You for clarity. May we not forget to work together as a team. I pray we will walk in the Spirit, not the flesh. Teach us how to have covenant, not contractual, love for each other. Most of all, help us remember why we married each other in the first place.

CHAPTER 12

How to Change Your Spouse

"A wife's prayers for her husband have a far greater effect on him than anyone else's, even his mother's. (Sorry, Mom.)"

—Stormie Omartian,
The Power of a Praying Wife

If you are struggling in your marriage, the best thing you can do is to pray over your spouse instead of criticizing him or her. I highly recommend *The Power of a Praying Wife* by Stormie Omartian. I started praying the prayers at the end of each chapter, and over time I saw changes. I am not sure if it was Andy or me who changed. I guess we both did.

When you start doing the right thing (covenant love) despite what your spouse is doing, it causes your spouse to change. He or she can't do things the same way because you are no longer doing things the same way. (The dysfunctional system breaks down.)

I also started praying scriptures back to God that directly targeted areas of concern in our marriage. Many times, I added Andy's name (and mine) to the verse in place of the pronouns. (By this time, I realized I was just as culpable.) You will be shocked at how powerful your prayers are when you do this.

If you are angry at your spouse, this may be hard at first. Keep praying, despite how you feel. Remember, your spouse is a daughter or son of the Most High and beloved to Him. God wants you to see your spouse the way He does.

Additionally, you are trading Satan's blueprint for God's perfect blueprint which means killing your flesh. Dave and Ann Wilson write in their book *Vertical Marriage*:

> And by the way, if your spouse won't surrender to God, then you do it. You can only control yourself. Ask God to work a miracle in your spouse. That is His job, not yours. (page 225)

You can never go wrong with prayer. It is the single most powerful weapon you have to restore your marriage.

THE POWER OF THE TONGUE

One of my friends has been counseling couples in distress for years. Over time she has noticed a pattern. Many times (not always) it is the wife who berates, cuts down, and humiliates her husband publicly and privately, destroying his self-worth, because she is angry about some type of bad behavior he continues in the marriage.

Many times, the anger is absolutely warranted, especially when there is sexual sin involved.* Pornography, adultery, sexting, etc. tends to bring out the worst in both parties. Clearly, the sexual sin must immediately stop, but so must the public and private humiliation of the other party (which many times is the husband) stop so healing can begin.

As much as a wife needs to be cherished and loved, a husband needs to be respected, even if he has acted horribly. Truthfully, this goes both ways. We all need love and respect!

Dave Wilson continues:

> A wife's words have power over her husband. Negative attitudes and words of "boo" do not motivate men, even if we deserve them. I'm not saying we can never hear criticism or correction because that is just a part of healthy communication in marriage. ... Men are motivated and empowered to change by cheering and by respect of their personal value as a man in the marriage apart from their duties. ... I promise you, booing and merciless critiquing just don't work. Why not try God's way of respect and see where it leads? (pages 136–137)

---

*While we have not personally dealt with sexual sin in our marriage, it is pervasive in this culture. If this is happening in your marriage, you need to get professional help. Sexual addiction must be brought to light; it breeds in the dark. True repentance includes confession, changed behavior, and a plan for recovery that includes enormous amounts of accountably and transparency. I highly recommend *Covenant Eyes* on all screens for starters and removing access to any other parties involved. It is important to cut out and/or block temptation while also getting into recovery. And start praying for God to break strongholds!

A critical spirit does nothing but destroy a marriage and make it next to impossible to have any hope of reconciliation. You are literally speaking death instead of life into your spouse when you say cruel and mean things. It furthers the destruction when you talk bad about your spouse to your kids. "The tongue has the power of life and death, and those who love it will eat its fruit" (Prov. 18:21).

Saying positive things to your spouse and others is one of the most powerful things you can do to change the tone of your marriage immediately. You must find something positive to say even if it is a small praise, at first. Someone has to break the unhealthy cycle. Be that godly person who steps in and says, "No more. It stops with me."

God has worked deeply in both Andy's and my lives to help us control what comes out of our mouths. We have learned the lesson that praise goes a lot further than criticism. No one likes to be "booed." Your spouse needs to know you are always on the same team while also having the freedom to step up and speak truth when needed.

THE POWER OF PRAYING FOR YOUR SPOUSE

If you want to address strongholds in your marriage, I suggest you learn how to pray. Here are some ideas for your personal prayer time. You can pray these prayers every day to protect your marriage or heal it. These prayers were inspired by

Stormie Omartian, but they are original prayers I have written for this book.

Prayer for Safety and Protection
Lord, I thank You right now for _____. I pray You would be with him/her wherever he/she goes (Josh. 1:9). Protect and keep him/her safe from harm. Keep him/her away from any kind of accident, sickness, or any other sort of destruction the evil one may have planned. I pray _____ would fear no evil as You are always with him/her, guiding and directing him/her to a straight path (Ps. 23:4). Give _____ discernment so as not to take any unnecessary risks or walk into a place of danger. Keep him/her safe from the Enemy who is out to kill, steal, and destroy (John 10:10). May all plans by whomever may wish to harm him/her be thwarted and canceled. God, I ask for You to be his/her refuge and strength, an ever-present help in trouble (Ps. 46:1).

Prayer for Direction
Help _____ and me to go in a direction that would be pleasing to You. Let us hear Your voice and be able to discern Your will for our marriage (Jer. 33:3). It is easy to get distracted with all the responsibilities that go with being a husband or wife. Show us how to juggle each responsibility with grace and wisdom, knowing that You alone can lead us properly. I pray You would be our example as You are our Shepherd, leading us beside still waters. I ask for our souls to be refreshed. I pray goodness and mercy would follow us all the days of our lives and we would dwell in Your house forever (Ps. 23).

Prayer for a Job Situation

I give _____'s job to you. I know that he/she may not like everything about it, but I pray he/she would not be weary in doing good (Gal. 6:9). I ask that _____ would be tenacious and not give up. Bless everything he/she puts his/her hands on; may he/she reap a harvest in due season (Gal. 6:9). May _____ always give careful and close attention to his/her responsibilities but not be out of balance. Help him/her not to be overbearing, irritable, or greedy. I also pray he/she would not have a propensity toward laziness. Instill in _____ a desire to be hardworking, diligent, and responsible with everything he/she has been given to do (Eccles. 9:10). Thank you, God, for providing for us. God, I ask that if _____ is not in the right occupation, You will show us what he/she is to be doing. I know that You gave him/her gifts that are irrevocable (Rom. 11:29). Help him/her to use these gifts to serve you as well as others. I pray nothing would be devoured, lost, or stolen from us (1 Pet. 5:8). I give everything we own to You, God. Help us to manage it wisely. I pray You would help us to be disciplined to give a tithe back to You so that we will be in complete obedience to Your will (Mal. 3:8–12).

Prayer for Help in Trials

God, I know You allow trials in our life for a reason, so I pray for You to be with _____ as he/she goes through difficult times. I pray we will cast our burdens on You and that You will sustain us in times of trouble (Ps. 55:2). Help me to love, support, and pray for _____ daily (Phil. 4:6–7). Show me how to be a godly wife/husband and the kind of spouse who is encouraging to him/her. Even though _____ may be hard-pressed on every side, do not let him/her be crushed. I pray he/she would not have a heart of despair. Help us to know that You will never abandon us in times of trouble (2 Cor. 4:8–9). Even when things don't look to be favorable, we can trust You are in control. Thank You, God, that those who trust and seek You will not be forsaken (Ps. 9:10).

Prayer for a Godly Spouse and Marriage

I pray that _____ will learn how to love me and I will learn how to love him/her (1 Cor. 13). I pray we will follow all the principles You have set before us so that we will have a healthy and vibrant marriage (Eph. 5:22–33). Help us to be quick to forgive each other so that things will not fester between us (Eph. 4:32). I pray _____ will seek You with a humble and teachable spirit (Prov. 5:33). Teach _____ how to be a godly person. Help me to be the kind of spouse who will lovingly support him/her and not tear him/her down (Prov. 31:10). Help us not to be critical or controlling. Instead, help us to love, honor, and respect each other as a brother or sister in Christ.

BREAKING STRONGHOLDS

Just to warn you, if you commit to praying boldy for your spouse and marriage, things may get a little worse before they get better. You may experience some extra "interruptions" when you start praying and asking God to break strongholds in your marriage. Don't be discouraged if this happens. Most of the time, it takes a trial for us to change our behavior.

God seems to do His best work through interruptions. They are never convenient; the timing always seems horrible, and it feels like the problems will last forever. However, God allows things to break down so He can rebuild them on His foundation, not ours.

If you want to make a powerful impact and jump-start your journey toward marital bliss, consider adopting the following four things.

1. **30-Day Challenge.** Your marriage will improve much faster if you will replace the nagging, criticism, control, or manipulation with encouragement and grace. Make your spouse the hero! For 30 days, say only positive and encouraging things to your spouse publicly and privately. (You need 30 days to break a habit.) Say nothing negative. Nada. I know this may be a struggle, but just close your mouth and breathe.

    Overlook the dirty socks he leaves on the floor, the hair wad she leaves in the shower, and anything else that bugs you. Catch your spouse doing good things and jump on that instead! Say "thank you" for his or her efforts. This doesn't mean you overlook really bad behavior. The point here is to have a kind and encouraging mouth.

2. **Practice Gratitude.** I highly recommend making a gratitude journal and actively listing the good things about not only your spouse, but what God has already done for you. The writers in the Bible constantly praise God through their lament. We need to do the same. This will help you to replace the bad tape in your head with good thinking. Do this alongside the 30-day challenge.
3. **Fasting.** Skip a meal or two or three … and replace the time with prayer. Or do a media fast or sugar fast if you can't go without food. Fasting breaks strongholds. You will see movement when you do this.
4. **Ministry.** Serve together. Turn outward, not inward. When you and your spouse work together doing ministry or volunteering, you bond together in Jesus. You are automatically united in a common goal. In turn, it resets the pattern in your marriage and makes it easier to unite in other ways as a couple.

When you turn inward, you become self-centered, and you tend to obsess. Obsession never leads to change. In fact, it made me sicker. Focus on other people's needs, and it will help you to be grateful for what you do have as a couple.

FINAL THOUGHTS ON PRAYER

I know what I am asking you to do is very hard. Some of you may not even know how to pray, so you struggle to find the right words. Furthermore, if you are having a difficult time in your marriage, the last thing you probably want to do is pray for your spouse. It goes against the flesh in every single way. Others of you would rather wallow in your pain; it feels good. I am an expert "wallower," so I understand. This should be your first clue: if it goes against your flesh, it's probably from heaven.

My question to you is, "What can you lose?" It costs nothing to pray. However, you have everything to gain. As Dave Wilson from FamilyLife Today says, "Why not try God's way and see where it leads?"

For me, it led to reconciliation after a seven-year estrangement.

REFLECTION

1. Do you have a critical spirit, especially as it relates to your spouse?
2. In what ways are you "booing" your spouse instead of cheering?
3. In what areas do you need to pray for your spouse daily?
4. Would you consider fasting to achieve a breakthrough? Pick a day.
5. What can you and your spouse do together to give back to others?

CHAPTER REVIEW

1. There is power in prayer.
2. Encouraging your spouse and expressing gratitude are two of the quickest ways to change your marriage immediately.
3. Fasting breaks strongholds.
4. Find a ministry to do together.

VERSES FOR SPIRITUAL WARFARE

Isaiah 58:6

"Is not this the kind of fasting I have chosen: to loose the chains of injustice and untie the cords of the yoke, to set the oppressed free and break every yoke?"

Jeremiah 29:12

"Then you will call on me and come and pray to me, and I will listen to you."

PRAYER

God, help me to truly believe prayer is the greatest weapon I have and that it will change our marriage. I call on You right now and ask You to give me the desire to pray and fast for my spouse and our marriage. Where the flesh is crying out in disdain, repulsion, or revenge, bring it back to align with Your Word. Enable me to love even though I have been deeply hurt. Show us how to put You first daily. Let us not get lazy or complacent about our relationship with You. Let us each run to You so we will meet in unity at Your throne. If my spouse is not interested in praying, I pray You would change his/her heart so that prayer becomes a passion and a way of life. Help us to be known for our prayer lives. I pray for big breakthroughs, so we know only You could have done it. I thank You for working in my marriage and bringing full healing to both of us. May we always give You the glory for any restoration we receive.

CHAPTER 13

Dreams Do Come True

"Dreams don't work unless you do."

—John C. Maxwell

It was the seventh Christmas we had spent estranged from my family. Frankly, Andy and I were tired of not being with those we loved. The loss was far greater than we ever dreamed it would be. We missed weddings, birthdays, holidays, and anniversaries for those seven years. Most of all, my kids missed seeing their cousins.

Andy and I felt God calling us back to my family, but we didn't know how to cross a broken bridge. Truthfully, the bridge was burned up and smoke was still rising from the ashes. By man's assessment, there was no going back. Too many things had been said and done that caused irreparable damage.

Nevertheless, I prayed that Christmas would be the last holiday away from them. I asked God for a miracle. I was secretly hoping He would do something that year, but nothing happened. I was a bit disappointed, but I could feel the Holy Spirit was working in some way. God had been impressing on my heart to not only pray but fast. Honestly, I thought it was a little dumb. I didn't see how starving myself was going to make any difference. (It's a miracle God hasn't just struck me dead yet!)

Reluctantly, I decided to listen and obey. I was desperate by this point and thought it couldn't hurt. So, I prayed and fasted on the first Monday and Tuesday of that next year.

I specifically asked God to talk to my dad in a dream. I was thinking that this might be the only way to reach him. I hate to admit this, but I prayed for a hellfire-and-brimstone dream. Yes, the working out of forgiveness does come in stages.

The next part of the story seems unreal, but I promise this is true: after seven years of being estranged, my father called three days after I fasted and prayed. He called that Friday. And why did he call? He had a dream.

God talked to my father in a dream just as I had prayed.

It wasn't a hellfire-and-brimstone dream, but it was still a dream. Instead of scaring my father into calling, God wooed him in a kind way. Probably a much better strategy.

My father dreamed Andy and I were sitting at the dining room table at his house with him and my mother. We were all eating dinner together, talking and smiling; it was a peaceful occasion.

After the dream, my father woke my mother in the middle of the night and told her I was coming home. I don't think she believed him. Instead, she brushed him off and told him to go back to sleep. She probably thought he had one too many servings of lasagna the night before.

When my dad called that Friday, it was nothing short of a miracle. Only one problem. After the call, I was angry because there were no real apologies. Over the next month, I struggled with moving forward. It had been seven long years. Why did it take that long for him to call? Furthermore, I didn't like being vulnerable. I was still hesitant to put myself out there and trust again.

God has a sense of humor because the week after that phone call, He put me in the hot seat. Our teaching leader from Bible Study Fellowship taught on forgiveness for 45 minutes. And let me tell you, that seat felt hot. Like really, literally hot. I was moving around the whole time feeling a strange sensation of heat. Weird, I know, but I am just telling you what happened. I couldn't possibly make this up.

After that incident, I knew I had to let go and trust God.

A month later, just as my father dreamed, Andy and I were at my parents' house, sitting at their dining room table and eating dinner, talking, and even smiling. It was then my father told us about his dream.

I was dumbfounded. I quickly relayed my part of the story—that I had prayed for God to speak to him in a dream. (I didn't exactly mention the hellfire-and-brimstone part.) When we put the time line together, we were in awe at how my father's dream occurred just days after I prayed and fasted.

All four of us knew only God could have orchestrated this. Jesus, our mediator, brokered our reconciliation through a dream. How many people can say that? The next part is even more amazing.

Months later, I found out my middle sister had been praying and fasting at the very same time—the first Monday and Tuesday in January. There was very little communication between us then, so there was no way we could have known what the other person was doing.

I would love to say I had this great faith when I prayed and fasted those two days, but that was not the case. Truthfully, it was my obedience to pray and fast that broke a generational stronghold of unforgiveness and estrangement.

It took seven long years for our reconciliation to happen.

Oddly, the estrangement from my parents redirected our marriage in a way I did not expect; it brought us closer together, not further apart. It ended up changing the dynamics of our marriage drastically. We were both hurting, and no one else understood the reason for our decision or the toll it was taking on us as a couple and as Christians. It forced us to work together as a team during a very difficult time. We had no idea that one problem would help resolve another problem.

God intervened in Andy's job situation. He now works for himself, so he is not gone all the time. Staying connected as a couple is a big priority for us. We make time for each other daily and talk about everything. There is no subject left untouched.

God also did a mighty work when it came to my health. Miraculously, my colon completely healed over time, and I never needed surgery. At my last colonoscopy, the doctor said there was a scar in one area, but if it weren't for that scar, he would never know I had Crohn's disease. What is even more miraculous is that I have weaned off all my medications. This is not normal for someone with Crohn's disease. Only a small percentage of people ever completely heal and get off prescription drugs. (Speaking of health, I did end up giving my kids cod liver oil when they were growing up. Did you know it is an awesome preventative for ear infections? Who knew? I guess Andy was right.)

Do we have a perfect marriage? No. But we apologize when we mess up. It doesn't take us days to admit our mistakes; it usually takes only hours. We know our tendencies and try to curb them. Most important of all, we attend church regularly and try to volunteer or do ministry together as a couple. (Right now, we are facilitators for a marriage class at our church.) We are now more approachable when things bother us, and we try to use appropriate conflict resolution skills. Both of us try very hard not to fall back into old destructive patterns.

More importantly, I am madly in love with the man I married 30 years ago. The key was forgiveness and working on ourselves individually. And leaving the rest to the Holy Spirit. I am so very grateful for my husband. He is such a kind and godly man. I don't have a hard time following him because he is a servant-leader.

An impossible job situation, a colon destined for an irreversible procedure, and a devastating family estrangement could have easily sent us spiraling into the abyss. Instead, God provided a new job for Andy, healed a diseased colon, and sent a miraculous dream. Through all the suffering, because of His great mercy, He united us as a couple. And in His abundant kindness, He also brought my extended family back into our lives.

Does this mean we live a pain-free, problem-free life? Not in the least bit. Sufferings from the past have given us strength as a couple to deal with present stress and future uncertainties. Whenever our lives are interrupted by trials, we look back and remember how Jesus has intervened on our behalf—not only on the cross, but also in other tangible ways.

When I don't see God work immediately, I remind myself I am shortsighted and that I can trust Him over the long haul. I put less faith in what I see and more hope in whom I know God is despite the circumstances. Don't lose hope if you are called to wait, whether it's for the healing of a broken relationship with a family member or with your spouse. Or even a physical healing. God does all the work in the waiting.

The job stress, health issues, and family estrangement made for a very hard seven years in our marriage journey. But God never abandoned us. Through it all, I came to understand God loves me, He is good, and I can trust Him.

HAS YOUR MARRIAGE BEEN INTERRUPTED?

If it hasn't happened already, sooner or later your life and marriage will be interrupted by something surprising and probably unpleasant. God promises us that we are going to have trials, and He even says to count it all joy when it happens (James 1:2). So, when your life is interrupted, what are you going to do? Will you run away and blame God because He didn't intervene at your appointed time? Or will you trust God even if it takes a long time for the problem to resolve?

As believers, we must understand the journey itself is important when facing a trial. Instead, many of us (me included) spend our time thwarting the process by manipulating the situation, taking control, running, or even blaming God for our misery. The truth is everything that happens on the journey serves to prepare us for the destination. When we refuse to let God work, we shortchange ourselves and even those around us.

Remember the Israelites who wandered the desert for 40 years? Perhaps you are supposed to be in a state of brokenness and waiting right now. Maybe God hasn't given you all the answers immediately because you need to learn over time. Maybe confession and repentance need to happen before you can move forward. (Not your spouse, but you.)

God is in the business of fixing broken things—even broken marriages. Allow Him to work in your own life and in your spouse's life. It is good to put on your spiritual glasses and remember that His purpose is far better than we can imagine. Your temporal suffering can bring glory to God if you surrender the situation to Him.

He knows what you have suffered. Just like silver and gold are purified by burning, you, too, are being refined through sometimes fiery trials. Those trials are burning off all the impurities.

In the waiting, rest in His complete and utter love for you. Commit to studying His Word until you know the truth. His truth will set you free. God can redeem even the worst interruptions in your marriage. Amos 9:9 says:

> For behold, I am commanding, and I shall shake and sift the house of Israel among all nations [and cause it to tremble] like grain is shaken in a sieve [removing the chaff], but not a kernel [of the faithful remnant] shall fall to the ground and be lost [from My sight]. (AMP)

REFLECTION

1. Did you know interruptions in your life and marriage are normal?
2. How are you handling the conflict God has allowed between you and your spouse?
3. What can you (not your spouse) do today to change the trajectory of your marriage? Get help, pray, fast, be kind?
4. In what ways do you need to obey God's Word, even when you don't understand why He is allowing suffering in your marriage?
5. Is God calling you to repentance? What do you need to confess?

CHAPTER REVIEW

1. God can redeem even the worst interruptions in your marriage.
2. Choosing to have a healthy marriage takes work, but it is worth it.
3. You can trust God with your long, hard journey.
4. Confession and repentance for your part will change your marriage.

VERSES FOR SPIRITUAL WARFARE

Isaiah 44:22

"I have swept away your offenses like a cloud, your sins like the morning mist. Return to me, for I have redeemed you."

Psalm 147:3

"He heals the brokenhearted and binds up their wounds."

PRAYER

God, I pray You would remove any thoughts of infidelity or divorce from our minds. I pray against pride, stubbornness, or blame that may be interfering with reconciliation. Let us be quick to confess when we are wrong. If we are called to suffer, I pray You would give us both the courage to face hard things together. Help us trust You when we feel like You are absent in our situation. Remind us that Your Word says You will never leave us or forsake us. Sweep away our offenses and remember them no more. Bind our broken hearts and heal us. God, I pray for complete redemption from our situation, no matter what has happened. Restore to us what the locusts have eaten. Renew our love so it reflects the marriage of Jesus to His bride (us).

APPENDIX

As I've shared, there were some specific things I did to heal my heart and find a deeper love for my husband. This final section is a compilation of suggestions I have recommended throughout the book. I have compiled them in one place so you can easily refer to them.

In fact, Andy and I still practice these. You can't do all of them at once, so choose where to start according to your situation. I do believe with my whole heart these suggestions will help you (like they helped us), because they are based on the truths of God's Word.

Matthew 5:48 says:

> You, therefore, will be perfect [growing into spiritual maturity both in mind and character, actively integrating godly values into your daily life], as your heavenly Father is perfect. (AMP)

This is an opportunity for you to integrate godly values daily in a practical way. Before you start balking, remember that Adam and Eve's rejection of truth are how we all got here in the first place. Marriage, just like everything worthwhile, takes work!

APPENDIX

SUGGESTIONS

Find faith. If you have not accepted Jesus as your Lord and Savior, it will be difficult to get traction in some of these other areas, especially in the area of forgiveness. These steps can only be accomplished with the supernatural power of God's Holy Spirit. If you don't know Jesus Christ, then it is time to reconsider your faith. Without His Spirit working within you, none of these suggestions will truly help.

You can surrender your life to Jesus right now by praying a simple prayer. God isn't concerned with your exact words; He is looking for a heart change (Rom. 10:9–10). It is the giving over of your life to Him that counts. You can pray something like this:

> Jesus, I come to You right now and thank You for dying on the cross for me. Please forgive me for all of my sins. I ask You to come into my heart and be Lord of my life. Thank You for giving me eternal life. Help me to live according to Your Word and be the kind of person You want me to be. In Jesus' name I pray, amen.

It is important to start attending a Bible-believing church and reading the Bible daily so you can grow. There is a lot to learn when you accept Christ as your Lord and Savior.

Pray and fast. Cry out to God in prayer and fasting. Ask Him to change your marriage. In the Bible, when God's children

APPENDIX

cried out to Him, He answered their prayers. Pray for changed hearts. Not just your spouse's heart, but yours too.

Show up as an adult. The silent treatment, rolling eyes, slamming doors, walking out of the room, yelling, pouting, sighing loudly, etc. are all childish behaviors children do. They are not appropriate behaviors for an adult. You are an adult now. Act like one.

Combat lies with scripture. Jesus quoted scriptures (truth) to Satan when tempted. This was an example for us. Take the time to identify the lies in your head and find scriptures that contradict them. Put them on note cards and say them every day. Insert your name or your spouse's name in the scriptures to make them more personal.

Give up control. Control, manipulation, and threats are not productive in any marriage. These are tactics Satan uses. Allow your spouse the space he or she needs. Work together as a team using healthy communication tools.

Set boundaries. Setting boundaries is one of the healthiest things you can do as a person. Learn how to say "no" when appropriate and be okay with yourself when you do it. (Mentally decide you can live without approval before it comes.) This also means letting go of people-pleasing. If you want to be fully known, you must be authentic.

APPENDIX

Encourage your spouse. Berating, criticizing, and "booing" are destructive. Have a kind mouth that is constantly praising. You can find something positive to say! It will change your marriage when you do this. Make your spouse the hero.

Forgive. God knows what happened to you. And He grieves with you. Instead of praying for revenge or having a critical spirit, pray blessings for those who hurt you. Release your spouse to God and let go.

Join a church, Sunday school class, and/or Bible study as a couple, if possible. Stay connected with your local church and find a smaller group of committed Christian friends. This will be one of the most transformative things you can do as a couple. The community time will keep you accountable and give you encouragement. If your spouse won't go, go alone.

Volunteer and/or go on mission trips as a couple. Get your mind off yourself. I found volunteering and mission trips to be great remedies for depression, anger, and self-absorption. When you are helping others, you are not thinking about your own situation. Big secret: When you work on building God's kingdom, not your own, it will bond you as a couple.

Worship. Play worship music to help you reprogram your mind. It is also a good remedy when you are feeling sad, rejected, angry,

APPENDIX

etc. Worship is a balm poured over all the raw places; it is a way to surrender your heart to God and drop everything in His lap.

Go to counseling. Go to counseling as a couple, if possible. If not, then go by yourself. If you don't want to use a counselor, try a pastor, or even a wise and trusted friend. A third party can make a huge difference by adding perspective.

Consider a marriage-focused class or small group. Andy and I help lead a marriage group at our church that is about 24 weeks long. We go through a workbook that is designed to help couples grow closer to each other and God. We get just as much out of it as those in the group!

Read and listen to good books and podcasts. It is important that you keep growing as an individual and as a couple. Read a marriage book together, listen to podcasts, and study the Bible regularly. Educate yourself on how to behave as a spouse. This stuff isn't taught in school, nor does it come naturally.

Live loved. It wasn't until I accepted God's love internally that I was able to truly love others. It took a long time to not only embrace God's love (pride) but to live as a loved person consistently.

Let go of self-pity. Let go of self-pity and replace it with gratitude. This is an important step in the healing process. As long as you are ruminating about what has happened to you, you will stay stuck. Envision a stop sign in your mind when it starts to happen. Get a gratitude journal and focus on the good things God has done for you.

Refer to the garden of Eden—The model God gave us in the garden of Eden is a great example of a healthy marriage environment before sin entered the world. Replicate the same themes in your home.

Work on yourself. At the end of the day, this is all you can control. You. Go back and deal with the baggage that you have brought into your marriage. You do your part. Let God deal with your spouse.

WHAT NEXT?

Now that you have read my story and been given a few tips, the rest is up to you. You can treat this as just a nice book with some funny stories or as a catalyst for change in your own life and marriage.

Becoming one with your spouse is not easy, especially when you each bring in a suitcase of hurts and unresolved issues from the past. Many times, the person you love the most is the one who also pushes your buttons and triggers shame and self-pity. The ones closest to us can bring out the worst in us.

Appendix

If this is happening to you, it is a good sign that you need to go back and heal. Maybe even forgive your spouse and those who hurt you long ago. You may need to set some strong boundaries with those who continue to hurt you.

Now is the time to fight lies with truth. I pray the Holy Spirit will empower you to face your difficulties head-on and become the person God designed you to be—whole, free, and healed.

Thank you for taking the time to read this book. If you would like to connect, here is my information.

Blog: www.momremade.com
Facebook group: Christian Family Living
Social media: @julieaplagens for Facebook, Pinterest, and Instagram
Email: momremade@gmail.com

APPENDIX

REFLECTION

1. Have you accepted Jesus as your Lord and Savior? Would you like to today?

2. Have you asked the Holy Spirit to give you the power to change?

3. What triggers you?

4. What is God calling you to remove from your life so you will be fully devoted to Him?

5. Who can you ask to be your accountability partner?

CHAPTER REVIEW

1. To have a good marriage, you need to keep growing as a person and as a couple.

2. If you are wounded, it is time to address the pain.

3. Don't forsake wise counsel.

4. God loves you, and He has a wonderful plan for you and your marriage.

APPENDIX

VERSES FOR SPIRITUAL WARFARE

Proverbs 15:22

"Plans fail for lack of counsel, but with many advisers they succeed."

Proverbs 12:15

"The way of fools seems right to them, but the wise listen to advice."

PRAYER

God, help me to be a good spouse. I know I cannot do this without You, so give me a new heart, mind, and soul that is penetrated by Your Holy Spirit. I confess to You the times I have been stubborn and resisted change. Forgive me for thinking that I can change my spouse. Only You can do this. I lay down every expectation I have for my spouse and my marriage. I give it all to You. Instead, I ask You to teach me how to pray for my spouse. I pray blessings on him/her all the days of his/her life. Help us to truly leave father and mother and cleave to each other as one. Unify us. Help us to see that we win together or lose together. Where we are not unified, help us to seek You first instead of bullying, withdrawing, or

Appendix

isolating. Let me be the first to say, "It stops with me." I thank You for helping us to deal with past wounds we have brought into our marriage. Give us a heart of forgiveness and repentance. Help us to give You all the glory for what You are going to do in our lives this day.

RECOMMENDED RESOURCES

1. *Anger: Facing the Fire Within* by June Hunt
2. *Boundaries in Marriage: Understanding the Choices That Make or Break Loving Relationships* by Dr. Henry Cloud and Dr. John Townsend
3. *Estranged: Finding Hope When Your Family Falls Apart* by Julie Plagens
4. *Forgiving What You Can't Forget* by Lysa TerKeurst
5. *Get Out of Your Head: Stopping the Spiral of Toxic Thoughts* by Jennie Allen.
6. *Is It Abuse? A Biblical Guide to Identifying Domestic Abuse and Helping Victims* by Darby A. Strickland
7. *The Jeremiah Study Bible* by David Jeremiah
8. *The Peacemaker: A Biblical Guide to Resolving Personal Conflict* by Ken Sande
9. *The Power of a Praying Wife* by Stormie O'Martian
10. *The Power of a Praying Husband* by Stormie O'Martin
11. *The Total Money Makeover: A Proven Plan for Financial Fitness* by Dave Ramsey
12. *Total Forgiveness* by R. T. Kendall
13. *Vertical Marriage* by Dave and Ann Wilson
14. *When to Walk Away: Finding Freedom from Toxic People* by Gary Thomas

SOURCE LIST

Holy Bible. New International Version, Zondervan Publishing House, 2011.

Hunt, June. *Anger: Facing the Fire Within.* Aspire Press, 2013.

Jeremiah, David. *The Jeremiah Study Bible.* Worthy Publishing, 2013.

Kendall, R. T. *Total Forgiveness.* Charisma House, 2007.

Omartian, Stormie. *The Power of a Praying Wife.* Harvest House Publishers, 2017.

Plagens, Julie. *Estranged: Finding Hope When Your Family Falls Apart.* Self-published, 2019.

Strickland, Darby A. *Is It Abuse?: A Biblical Guide to Identifying Domestic Abuse and Helping Victims.* P&R Publishing, 2020.

TerKeurst, Lysa. *Forgiving What You Can't Forget.* Thomas Nelson, 2020.

TerKeurst, Lysa. *It's Not Supposed to Be This Way.* Nelson Books, 2018.

Wilson, Dave and Ann. *Vertical marriage: The One Secret That Will Change Your Marriage.* Zondervan, 2018.

ABOUT THE AUTHOR

Julie is a wife, mother, author, teacher, and blogger. Before she married, she taught speech, drama, and English for three years in the Richardson Independent School District. After she married, she became a stay-at-home mom and homeschooled her kids for a short stint. Julie has volunteered for many years locally and in South Texas doing VBS, food distribution, and door-to-door witnessing.

Now that her children are grown, Julie works intermittently for her husband, writes, and speaks. When Julie is not talking about marriage, family relationships, and mom life, she is shar-ing helpful tips on her blog. Julie lives with her husband of 31 years in Dallas, Texas.

IF YOU ENJOYED THIS BOOK, PLEASE CONSIDER SHARING IT WITH OTHERS.

Recommend this book personally to friends and family, as well as to those in your small group, book club, workplace, and classes.

Mention the book in a blog post or on Twitter, or upload a photo of the cover with your positive review to Instagram, Facebook, and Pinterest.

Connect with the author on Facebook to express your appreciation for the book's message and, perhaps, how it had a positive effect on your life.

Order a copy of the book for someone you know who would be challenged and encouraged by its message.

Look for the book on Amazon.com and leave a positive review.

And visit us to see the many other books, products, and publishing services we offer.

CreativeEnterprisesStudio.com

1507 SHIRLEY WAY, SUITE A
BEDFORD, TX 76022-6737
ACREATIVESHOP@AOL.COM

www.ingramcontent.com/pod-product-compliance
Lightning Source LLC
Chambersburg PA
CBHW032114090426
42743CB00007B/347